N. W. HEREFORD
RT. 2 BOX 213-A
DOBSON, N.C.
27017

N. Hereford

American Antiques

American Antiques

Norman Hudson

South Brunswick and New York: A. S. Barnes and Company
London: Thomas Yoseloff Ltd.

A. S. Barnes and Co., Inc.
Cranbury, New Jersey 08512

Thomas Yoseloff Ltd.
108 New Bond Street, London WIY OQX, England

ISBN 0-498-07678-4
Printed in the United States of America

Contents

Preface

This book is dedicated to that wonderful group of Americana lovers, collectors, decorators and dealers who have become interested in the many and varied items of long ago that have passed from family to family and to friend and for various reasons to the Auction sale.

It is published in the hope that it will help its readers to familiarize themselves with the various types, styles and values of Antique furnishings found in New England.

Each item contains four salient features: 1. The actual photograph of each piece (*the most critical and important ingredient of any description of an antique item*); 2. A quick word description; 3. The approximate time of its manufacture; 4. The date of sale followed by the price at Auction based on condition and rarity. For price appreciation/comparison all items are segregated first by date of sale.

One of the best methods of determining the value of an Antique is to attend a country auction. There a consistently knowledgeable group of people, both collector and dealer alike, compete in determining the price of an item on-the-spot. Under most circumstances the price will be its value to the collector or for resale. It's most unlikely that an excessive amount will be bid for any item at the legitimate auction.

Acknowledgements

I am greatly indebted to Richard W. Withington, one of New England's most prominent auctioneers, who made available his vast records and files of past auction material, without which it would have been impossible to produce "American Antiques." His help and diligent study of past records to learn the selling price of each of the many illustrated items was indeed a monumental task. "Dick" is to be congratulated on the accuracy of his records and his phenomenal memory of past auctions. Dick's wife Mary also deserves many thanks for the help she supplied in cleaning up the mess I undoubtedly left on my many visits to research the material.

The generous assistance of Daniel Hingston deserves grateful recognition. Without his articulate and copious knowledge of Antiques, their origin, use and description, I would have been unable to provide the vast amount of valuable descriptive data. "Dan" is truly a walking encyclopedia on the subject of Antiques. His storehouse of knowledge is so vast he is able to tell in a few seconds time, the origin, probable date and yes, come very close to the value of any Antique item. I will never be able to fully express my gratitude for the hours Dan spent checking over my material. Incidently Dan is the man responsible for the smooth running feature of all the wonderful Withington auctions.

A note of thanks belongs here to my son Jeffery, who spent long hours typing and retyping all the text for these many pages and managed to decipher my illegible scribble without error.

Deserving of prominent mention on this page, too, is my wife Connie, who lived in a half-house for months with papers, photographs and proofs scattered over most of the rooms. She helped me collate the many pieces of different material into a useful whole. Without her patience and understanding I would surely have been unable to complete "Antiques At Auction."

Photography by
Robert Swenson
Concord, New Hampshire

At the Auction

It's five minutes before ten o'clock, the two hundred chairs under the tent have long since been reserved by bags of food, knitting, paper signs, an empty carton, a piece of clothing, a neatly tied rope, or the body of the person who will sit attentively for the next six or seven hours.

The caterer has already sold 64 cups of coffee; if the day is chilly, he may have sold twice that many plus a few boxes of pastry and other goodies . . . the audience is at high pitch. Thirty-seven late arrivals are suddenly looking for seats and finding them taken. A sweet little old lady is crawling under a large table, the maker's imprint is being studied on countless plates, pitchers and jugs. Three people are trying to determine the use of the board filled with neatly spaced holes. A stranger to the scene would probably wonder why seven apparently sane people would be looking at the bottom of the drawers from a pretty maple slant top desk, sliding their hands over its side, dumping it over, inspecting its feet, back and hinges, and the stranger would be content to guess that the seven must surely be doctors on a holiday who for the moment forgot the desk is not human. At sixty seconds before ten we find plenty of standees on the circumference of the excitement and from the surrounding area people are hurrying now toward the center of the tent's shelter. Someone says 'what are we waiting for' — and on a raised platform you'll find a smiling face industriously sizing up the attendance, because no one at this particular moment has more interest in who's among the crowd than Richard W. Withington, "Dick" to his friends.

It's ten o'clock and Dick is calling for attention and quiet. Many times before he has been "King for the Day." His followers seated before him make up as diverse a group as one could find. Doctors, veterinarians, engineers and auto mechanics, restaurateurs and butchers, collectors and dealers all are assembled for a day under the tent.

Alright, let's get started, who will make it thirty-five . . . and another of "Dick's" Auctions is underway.

American Antiques

Lowboys, Highboys & Bureaus

Queen Anne walnut lowboy, cut corner top, circa 1750

1964 June $1,000.00

Mahogany inlaid swell front bureau with simple French feet and scrolled apron, circa 1800

1964 June $425.00

Queen Anne curly maple highboy, typical of Connecticut, unusual spiral corner columns, circa 1760-80

1964 June $2,600.00

Small Hepplewhite mahogany inlaid sideboard with matched veneer and string inlay, circa 1780

1964 June $530.00

Block front chest-on-chest, mahogany, restored bonnet and feet, circa 1760-80
1964 July $1,100.00

Choice Chippendale mahogany block-front bureau in untouched condition, note top shaped to conform with blocking in drawers, circa 1750-80

1964 June $5,800.00

Small Hepplewhite sideboard, string inlay with original brasses, circa 1780-1800
1964 July $750.00

Cherry four drawer bureau with ogee bracket base and thumbnail molded top, circa 1760
1964 July $975.00

Swell front bureau, mahogany with satinwood inlay, circa 1780-1800
1964 July $360.00

Chippendale maple oxbow bureau with bracket base, circa 1780

        1964 September $625.00

Cherry chest-on-chest with rounded quarter columns and ogee bracket base, circa 1750-80

        1964 September $1,200.00

Queen Anne mahogany highboy with bonnet top, restored bonnet and legs, circa 1760-80

        1964 July $1,300.00

Maple graduated four drawer chest with bracket base and thumbnail molded top, circa 1780

1964 September $400.00

Curly maple five drawer graduated chest with bracket base and molded top, circa 1780

1964 September $375.00

Early Queen Anne highboy, maple with burled walnut veneered drawer fronts, circa 1720

1964 October $1,575.00

Chippendale four drawer chest, walnut, ogee feet, unusual molded top, circa 1760

1964 October $600.00

Miniature pine four drawer chest with original graining 20" high, circa 1800
1964 October $425.00

Small maple chest of five graduated drawers with bracket base and molded top, circa 1780

1965 March $400.00

Small Queen Anne slipper foot low boy in cherry, circa 1720-50
1964 October $3,600.00

Sheraton four drawer bureau, mahogany with maple drawer fronts, circa 1800-20
1965 March $400.00

Chippendale Applewood oxbow chest, with bracket feet and original brasses, circa 1750-80

1965 March $1,200.00

Cherry Queen Anne three drawer chest on frame with writing slide, circa 1740-60

1965 June $550.00

Queen Anne cherry highboy with star inlay in top drawer, circa 1750

1965 March $850.00

Chippendale mahogany oxbow bureau with ogee bracket base, circa 1750-80

1965 June $725.00

Hepplewhite mahogany Baltimore side-
board with serpentine front and fine inlay,
circa 1780-1800
                    1965 June $900.00

Mahogany sideboard with brass rail and
paw feet, circa 1800
                    1965 August $200.00

Cherry chest with six graduated drawers
with ogee bracket base and fluted quarter
columns, circa 1750-80
                    1965 June $1,000.00

Rare Chippendale mahogany inlaid gen-
tleman's wardrobe in three parts with ogee
bracket base, circa 1750-80
                    1965 August $450.00

*Queen Anne mahogany base to highboy
with excellent shell carving, circa 1750*
1965 August $430.00

*Sheraton swell front bureau, fine inlay,
mahogany, circa 1800-20*
1965 October $700.00

*Queen Anne maple chest on frame, circa
1750-80*
1965 October $1,125.00

Queen Anne maple highboy, circa 1750
1965 October $1,775.00

*French provincial fruitwood bureau, circa
1780*

> 1965 November $250.00

*Four drawer Sheraton cherry bureau with
rare whalebone drawer pulls, circa 1815*

> 1966 February $420.00

*Tall curly maple chest of six graduated
drawers with molded top and plume carving on bracket base, circa 1750-80*

> 1966 February $800.00

*Graduated six-drawer cherry chest, circa
1780*

> 1966 March $700.00

Hepplewhite mahogany serpentine front sideboard, circa 1780

1966 March $675.00

Queen Anne Birch highboy with five fan carvings, circa 1750
Probably made in Vermont; note high pad feet

1966 March $1,450.00

Six graduated drawer pine chest with old graining, hardware replaced, circa 1780

1966 March $575.00

Inlaid mahogany Hepplewhite serpentine front sideboard with center drawer containing butlers desk, circa 1780

1966 May $900.00

Four drawer maple chest with bracket base, top has 3" overhang, circa 1780
1966 May $650.00

Five drawer curly maple graduated chest with molded top and bracket base, circa 1780
1966 May $650.00

Hepplewhite mahogany inlaid bow front bureau, circa 1780-1800
1966 May $340.00

Queen Anne walnut lowboy with concave block center drawer, note scrolls on legs, probably Rhode Island, circa 1720-50
1966 May $3,500.00

Tall birch chest of six graduated drawers with Queen Anne base and molded top, circa 1760

1966 July $950.00

Curly maple Queen Anne highboy with fan carving, circa 1750

1966 July $1,850.00

Hepplewhite cherry bow front bureau with French feet — signed J. Feltt

1966 July $700.00

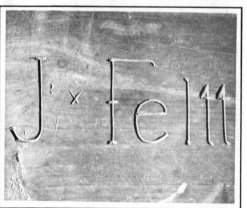

Baltimore tidewater sideboard, circa 1820
1966 July $350.00

Queen Anne maple highboy, circa 1750
1966 July $1,550.00

Curly maple highboy in untouched condi-
tion, hidden document drawer in upper
molding, circa 1730-50
1966 July $2,500.00

Queen Anne dressing table, mahogany
veneer, circa 1750
1966 July $425.00

Maple drawer chest with serpentine top and ogee bracket base, note double fan in apron, circa 1750-60

1966 August $4,100.00

Maple Queen Anne highboy, circa 1750
1966 July $2,350.00

Maple six drawer chest, circa 1780
1966 August $550.00

Maple four drawer chest, circa 1780
1966 August $450.00

Rare Chippendale mahogany scroll-top.
Philadelphia highboy, circa 1750-80
1966 August $11,000.00

Early Queen Anne highboy, found in shed
with legs cut off, circa 1740
1966 August $1,000.00

Curly maple chest on chest with ogee bracket base, New England, circa 1760-80
1966 August $1,825.00

Curly maple chest on chest with ogee bracket base, large fan carving in top and small fan on apron, circa 1760-80
1966 August $4,700.00

Maple four drawer chest with molded top, circa 1780

1966 October $320.00

Six drawer maple Chippendale chest, circa 1780

1966 October $350.00

Maple Hepplewhite four drawer chest, circa 1800

1966 November $210.00

Cherry four drawer chest with fluted corners and inlaid drawers, base not original, circa 1800

1966 October $170.00

Pine two drawer blanket chest made to simulate four drawer chest, circa 1760

1966 November $160.00

Queen Anne curly maple highboy with fan carving in base, circa 1750
1967 January $2,250.00

Four drawer cherry chest with serpentine top, circa 1780
1967 January $375.00
a. Liverpool pitchers   each $40.00

Cherry bow front bureau with French feet and rare whale bone pulls, circa 1780-1800
1967 January $550.00

Cherry Queen Anne highboy, note short legs, circa 1760-75

1967 March $2,800.00

Cherry bow front bureau with French feet, circa 1780-1800

1968 January $550.00

Sheraton bureau of birch and birdseye maple, circa 1820

1967 November $270.00

Seven drawer cherry chest, brasses replaced, circa 1780

1967 March $750.00

Curly maple Queen Anne highboy, shows no trace of ever having brasses, circa 1750-1780

1968 January $3,400.00

Queen Anne lowboy of walnut with Spanish feet, circa 1740-60

1968 January $4,700.00

Curly maple Hepplewhite four drawer chest, circa 1780-1800

1968 January $600.00

Chippendale six drawer chest of curly maple, circa 1780
>> 1968 January $1,300.00

Queen Anne walnut lowboy with drake feet, hardware replaced, circa 1780
>> 1968 February $5,300.00

Six drawer maple chest with bracket base hardware replaced, circa 1780
>> 1968 February $650.00

Mahogany Chippendale chest with ogee bracket base and bow front, circa 1780-1800
>> 1968 February $575.00

Queen Anne maple highboy, with bandy legs, circa 1750-70

1968 February $3,100.00

Pine and maple Queen Anne highboy with oak legs, circa 1760

1968 March $1,300.00

Mahogany four drawer chest with French feet, circa 1780-1800

1968 February $675.00

Hepplewhite mahogany bow front bureau with pin wheel carving in apron, diamond inlay across top, circa 1780-1800
1968 March $925.00

Cherry bow front bureau with bracket base, circa 1780
1968 April $625.00

Maple and walnut Queen Anne highboy with original hardware, circa 1740-60
1968 April $2,800.00

Maple Chippendale chest-on-chest, circa 1780
1968 April $1,375.00

Maple chest with four drawers, mahogany and curly maple inlay, circa 1780
1968 May $390.00

Chippendale chest-on-chest, wavy birch, circa 1780
1968 May $1,550.00

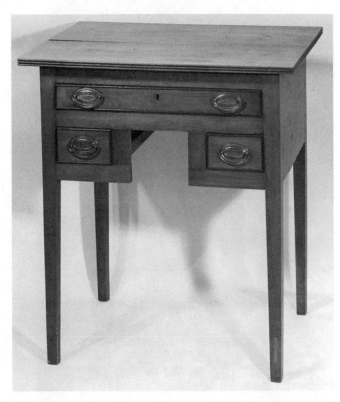

Hepplewhite cherry dressing table with tapered legs, circa 1780-1800
1968 May $160.00

Sheraton four drawer chest, maple and mahogany inlaid drawer fronts, circa 1800-1820

1968 May $330.00

Chippendale cherry oxbow bureau with ogee bracket base, circa 1760

1968 July $1,250.00

Chippendale graduated maple chest, circa 1780

1968 July $775.00

Queen Anne curly maple highboy with spliced feet, circa 1740-60

1968 July $1,025.00

Chippendale walnut four drawer chest ogee bracket base and fluted quarter columns, circa 1760-80

1968 August $600.00

Mahogany Chippendale inlaid bureau with serpentine front, note chamfered corners, circa 1760-80

1968 August $675.00

Seven drawer graduated cherry chest with bracket base and molded top, circa 1760-1780

1968 August $975.00

Four drawer cherry bureau with loop and tassel inlay at top, French feet and fan inlay in drawer corners, circa 1780-1800

1968 August $725.00

Hepplewhite mahogany bow-front bureau, circa 1780-1800

1968 August $575.00

Mahogany Sheraton four drawer bureau, circa 1800-20

1968 August $350.00

English, lacquered chest on frame with ball feet, circa 1740-60

1968 August $425.00

Sheraton dressing table, mahogany, attributed to Appleton of Salem, circa 1800-1830

1968 August $825.00

Sheraton mahogany small side board, circa 1820-40

1968 August $800.00

Maple Chippendale chest of six graduated drawers, fan carving on top drawer, circa 1780

1968 October $1,650.00

Six drawer graduated Chippendale cherry chest, circa 1780

1968 October $1,225.00

Mahogany bow front bureau, feet restored, circa 1780-1800

1968 October $1,200.00

*Curly maple five drawer chest, small size
with dovetail bracket base, circa 1760-80
1968 October $625.00*

*Chippendale maple chest-on-chest with
ogee bracket base and molded top, circa
1760-80*

1968 October $4,000.00

*Maple six drawer graduated chest, circa
1760-80*

1968 November $875.00

Curly maple Chippendale four drawer
chest, circa 1760-80
                    1969 January $500.00

Queen Anne curly maple highboy attributed to the Dunlap family, circa 1760
              1968 October $4,300.00

Sheraton mahogany and cherry sideboard
with small proportions, circa 1800-20
                    1969 January $600.00

Queen Anne cherry highboy
with fan carving, circa 1740-60

     1969 January $500.00

Queen Anne maple highboy, circa 1740-60
   1969 January $2,350.00

Chippendale cherry chest with four graduated drawers and bracket base, circa
1760-80

     1969 February $725.00

Mahogany Hepplewhite bow front bureau
with inlay, circa 1780-1800

1969 February $550.00

Queen Anne cherry highboy with pineapple carving on top and bottom drawers,
circa 1740-60

1969 February $1,600.00

Hepplewhite mahogany side board, circa
1780-1800

1969 March $825.00

Sheraton mahogany side board, circa 1800-
1820

1969 February $500.00

Queen Anne maple highboy base with fan carving, circa 1740-60
> 1969 March $520.00

Hepplewhite cherry four drawer bureau, circa 1780-1800
> 1969 May $450.00

Maple four drawer chest with bracket base and molded top, circa 1780
> 1969 March $900.00

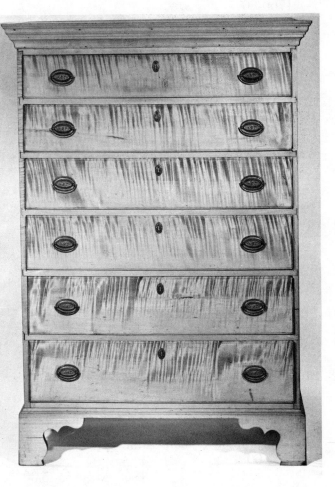

Curly maple six drawer tall chest, circa 1780
> 1969 September $1,275.00

Four drawer blanket chest in pine, circa 1760-80

1969 June $230.00

Queen Anne highboy, circa 1740-60
1969 September $5,800.00

English oak Queen Anne lowboy, circa 1740-60

1969 May $525.00

Cherry bow front bureau, circa 1780
1969 September $900.00

Mahogany chest with seven drawers, circa 1840

1969 September $425.00

Panel front chest, circa 1680-1700
1969 September $3,300.00
a. Pewter pitchers $50.00 and $135.00
b. Burl bowl $340.00

Cherry four drawer bureau, serpentine top, ogee feet, circa 1760-80
1969 September $1,600.00

Marquetry inlaid three drawer chest, circa

	1969 September	$450.00
a. Candelabra	pr.	$230.00
b. Tureen		$25.00

Three drawer French Provincial chest
1969 September $1,200.00

Italian chest elaborately carved
1969 October $275.00

English mahogany straight front bureau with French feet, circa 1800-20
1970 January $250.00

Base to Queen Anne highboy, circa 1740-1760
1970 January $625.00

New Hampshire chest on chest attributed to the Dunlap family, circa 1780
1970 January $4,600.00

Maple five drawer graduated chest with bracket base and molded top, circa 1780
1970 January $625.00

Hepplewhite mahogany "D" shaped side-board, circa 1800
> 1970 January $1,000.00

Mahogany bow-front bureau with bracket feet, circa 1800
> 1970 January $450.00

Cherry six drawer chest on Queen Anne frame, frame restored, circa 1760-80
> 1970 February $525.00

French Marquetry commode with ormolu trim and maple top, circa 1800
> 1970 February $275.00

Pine four drawer bureau with painted and grained ogee bracket base, fluted quarter columns, circa 1780

1970 February $400.00

Salem four drawer mahogany wood inlay bureau, circa 1800

1970 February $400.00

Chippendale maple five drawer chest with bracket base and thumbnail molded top, circa 1780

1970 March $750.00

Sheraton mahogany Salem server, circa 1820

1970 March $475.00

Sheraton mahogany inlaid four drawer bureau, Salem type, circa 1800-20
1970 March $375.00

Chippendale cherry four drawer chest with fluted quarter columns and ogee feet, circa 1760-80
1970 March $825.00

Chippendale maple six drawer chest with dovetail bracket base, circa 1760-80
1970 March $825.00

Cherry Hepplewhite six drawer chest containing a bonnet drawer, circa 1800
1970 March $550.00

Chests

Pilgrim period panelled and carved oak blanket chest, note initials B. P., circa 1670-1700

1964 June $380.00

Large oak and pine European sideboard with extensive panelling and carving, 7' 9" long X 39" high, circa 1680

1964 September $700.00

Pewter pitchers, left & right

pr. $110.00

Two pair of Candlesticks

each pr. $55.00

Funnel

$20.00

Large deep dish

$165.00

Charger

$85.00

Pair of small porringers

pr. $60.00

Measure

$21.00

Pennsylvania dowery chest with three drawers and painted panels, ogee bracket base, dated 1773

1964 July $1,200.00

Two drawer pine blanket chest with bracket base, unusual moldings, circa 1760-80

1964 October $250.00

Shaker three drawer chest with work table slide, circa 1830

1964 October $557.00

Connecticut oak four drawer chest with split spindles, circa 1680-1720

1965 June $1,150.00

Pine three drawer chest with ball feet, panelled front and sides, circa 1680-1720
1965 June $550.00

Early tall chest in pine with five graduated drawers and bracket base molded top, old red paint, circa 1760
1965 August $340.00

Chest of four graduated drawers in old red paint, circa 1790
1965 August $240.00

Small nine drawer chest, with ball feet, circa 1700
1966 March $325.00

One drawer blanket chest with ball feet, circa 1700

1966 July $650.00

Thirty-nine drawer apothecary chest with separate cupboard top, circa 1790-1810
1966 March $200.00

New England linen fold chest, circa 1700
1966 July $1,250.00

Small English oak ball foot chest, circa 1700

1966 July $230.00

Pine two drawer blanket chest with bracket base, circa 1700-20

1966 July $350.00

Pine two drawer blanket chest, turnip feet, circa 1720

1966 August $625.00

Small single drawer blanket chest with turning feet, circa 1720

1966 August $400.00

Harvard bookcase, made in Vermont, each section lifts off, circa 1820

1966 August $550.00

One drawer pine blanket chest with ball feet, circa 1700

1966 August $1,250.00

Pine linen fold blanket chest, initials probably those of owner — some scratch carving, circa 1680-1720

1966 August $500.00

Oak single drawer blanket chest with panel front and pine lid, circa 1700-20

Twelve drawer pine spice chest, circa 1930-1850

1966 November $90.00

Carved oak chest, circa 1700

1968 April $360.00

Single drawer blanket chest, circa 1750
1968 July $405.00
a. Pine ball foot Bible box, circa 1720
1968 July $275.00

Single drawer pine blanket chest, circa
1720
1968 July $725.00
a. Slip ware pot   *$55.00*
b. Ball foot Bible box   *$110.00*
c. Rush light   *$75.00*

Single drawer ball foot blanket chest, circa
1720
1968 July $1,525.00

Pine linen fold chest dated 1699, circa 1700
1968 July $450.00
a. Hat, circa 1800
1968 July $5.00
b. Linsey Woolsey, circa 1820
1968 July $110.00
c. Pierced tin lantern
1968 July $115.00

a. *Slat back mushroom arm chair, circa 1720*
1968 July $550.00

b. *Queen Anne looking glass, circa 1740-60*
1968 July $105.00

c. *Tin sconces, circa 1780*
1968 July each $90.00

d. *Painting of Gentlemen, circa 1820*
1968 July $250.00

e. *Two drawer pine blanket chest, circa 1700*
1968 July $925.00

f. *Bannister back side chair, circa 1720*
1968 July $550.00

Five drawer ball foot chest with painted decoration, circa 1700
1968 July $825.00

a. *Queen Anne mirror, circa 1720-40*
1968 July $275.00

b. *Bell bottom candle sticks, circa 1720*
1968 July pr. $170.00

Five drawer ball foot chest, pine and maple, circa 1700

1968 July $2,250.00

a. Painting of a Lady, done in pastel, circa 1820

1968 July $375.00

b. Sconce at left $80.00

Chippendale walnut two drawer blanket chest with ogee feet, circa 1760-80
1968 August $225.00

Maple two drawer blanket chest with dovetailed base, circa 1780
1968 November $180.00

Single drawer blanket chest with double arch molding, circa 1740-60
                              1969 March $550.00

One drawer blanket chest, circa 1680-1700
                    1969 September $1,400.00

a. Bible box, circa 1680
                              $700.00

Chest on frame in single unit, circa 1680
                    1969 September $2,000.00

a. Hanging wall box with drawer, circa 1720
                              $225.00

One drawer blanket chest with ball feet, circa 1720

                1969 September $1,700.00

a. Bennington Pitchers   *Left* $130.00
                         Right $140.00
b. Bennington Bowl $130.00

English oak dower chest, circa 1740
           1970 February $400.00

Desks & Secretaries

Chippendale mahogany serpentine-front desk with ball and claw feet, circa 1780
1964 June $700.00

Sheraton mahogany inlaid secretary with cylinder front desk, circa 1830
1964 June $650.00

Curly maple slant top desk, ogee bracket feet, circa 1780
1964 June $1,000.00

Chippendale maple slant top desk, circa 1780-1800

1964 July $390.00

Small maple slant top desk, circa 1750-60
1964 July $1,200.00

Chippendale cherry secretary with broken arch top and sunburst carvings, circa 1750-1780

1964 October $1,800.00

Chippendale ball and claw foot ox bow slant top desk, mahogany, three drawers in bottom section, has unusually high legs, circa 1750-80

1964 October $1,550.00

Hepplewhite mahogany secretary with blind doors in top and French feet, original brasses, circa 1780-1800

1965 March $850.00

Cherry slant top desk, replaced hardware, circa 1780-1800

1965 March $575.00

Maple slant top desk with Queen Anne feet and sunburst carving, circa 1750

1965 June $825.00

Chippendale mahogany serpentine front slant top desk with ball and claw feet, circa 1750-80

1965 August $1,150.00

Hepplewhite mahogany inlaid secretary with glazed panelled doors, circa 1780-1800
1965 August $1,300.00

Mahogany Hepplewhite inlaid break front secretary (reputed to be of the family of Eleazer Wheelock, founder of Dartmouth College), circa 1780

1965 August $2,200.00

Slant top cherry Chippendale desk, circa 1750-80

          1965 October $725.00

Chippendale mahogany Serpentine front slant top desk with ogee bracket base, circa 1750-80

          1965 November $800.00

Cherry slant top desk with ogee bracket base and fine interior, circa 1750-80

          1965 November $900.00

36" Maple slant top desk with plain interior, circa 1780

          1966 January $600.00

Chippendale cherry slant top desk with fine interior and ogee bracket base, circa 1750-80

1966 February $675.00

36" Maple slant top desk with bracket base, plain interior, circa 1780

1966 May $430.00

Marquetry desk containing secret well, circa 1760

1966 May $275.00

Cherry slant top desk with unusual bracket base, circa 1780-1800

1966 May $570.00

Chippendale bonnet top ox bow secretary with ball and claw feet, unusual panelled doors, circa 1750-80

1966 July $1,850.00

Early pine two drawer desk, circa 1720

1966 July $700.00

a. Lighting fixture $310.00
b. Inkwell $210.00

Hepplewhite mahogany inlaid tambour desk with French feet, circa 1780-1800

1966 August $525.00

Small curly maple slant top desk with fine interior, circa 1760

1966 August $2,000.00

Maple slant top desk hardware not original, circa 1780

1966 August $825.00

Secretary Vermont graining, knobs not original, circa 1780

1966 August $750.00

Cherry ox bow slant top desk with ogee bracket base, circa 1770-80

1966 October $1,050.00

Chippendale maple secretary with panel doors, circa 1780

1966 August $1,075.00

Maple slant top desk, base not original, circa 1780

1966 November $555.00

Chippendale mahogany serpentine slant top desk with ogee bracket base, circa 1780
1966 November $885.00

Maple slant top desk with plain interior, circa 1780
1967 January $550.00

Pine schoolmasters desk, circa 1800-20
1966 November $140.00

English Chippendale mahogany Bombe-front slant top desk, circa 1750-80
1967 January $300.00

Cherry slant top desk, feet replaced, circa 1780

1967 March $525.00

Birch 36" desk with double step interior, Hardware replaced, circa 1780

1967 November $775.00

a. Pair of Queen Anne brass candlesticks, circa 1740

1967 November pr. $80.00

Hepplewhite mahogany inlaid secretary with French feet, circa 1790-1810

1967 November $975.00

Curly maple 34½" high Chippendale desk, circa 1770-80

1968 January $2,000.00

Pilgrim period slant top desk on frame, circa 1700-20

1968 January $1,500.00

Curly maple slant top desk with fine interior, circa 1760-80

1968 February $1,850.00

Chippendale cherry slant top desk, circa 1780

1968 February $825.00

Mahogany Hepplewhite blind door secretary, circa 1780-1800

1968 March $700.00

Mahogany Chippendale oxbow desk with ball and claw feet, circa 1760-80

1968 March $1,100.00

Mahogany Sheraton secretary with blind doors, circa 1800-20

1968 April $600.00

Maple 36" slant top desk, hardware replaced, circa 1780

1968 April $1,000.00

Chippendale mahogany slant top desk, feet have been replaced, circa 1780

1968 May $575.00

Sheraton mahogany cylinder top desk, circa 1800-20

1968 August $725.00

Schoolmasters desk on frame, circa 1780-1800

1968 August $220.00

a. Captain's Chair extra high, newly decorated, circa 1800-20

1968 August $90.00

Sheraton secretary, birch and curly maple with heavy legs and carving, circa 1820-40
1968 July $280.00

Chippendale walnut slant top desk, circa 1780

1968 July $1,075.00

Chippendale walnut slant top desk with fine interior, shell carving on center door, circa 1760-80

1968 August $1,025.00

Hepplewhite, cherry with maple and mahogany inlay secretary, circa 1780

1968 October $1,300.00

Hepplewhite mahogany slant top desk, French feet, circa 1780-1800

1968 August $725.00

Hepplewhite cherry slant top desk, circa 1780-1800

1968 October $1,475.00

Shaker ladies desk, circa 1800-60
1969 January $650.00

Cherry Chippendale slant top desk with secretary top, circa 1760-80
1968 November $1,475.00

Chippendale mahogany slant top desk with fine blocked interior and four secret drawers, inset shows secret compartments, circa 1760-80

1969 January $1,600.00

Shaker elders desk, circa 1800-60
1969 January $1,600.00

Empire fall front desk, circa 1800-20
1969 February $525.00

*Hepplewhite mahogany inlaid secretary
with tambour doors, circa 1780-1800*
1969 February $1,200.00

Chippendale cherry slant top desk with fan carved interior, circa 1760-80
1969 February $925.00

Chippendale birch slant top desk with ogee bracket base and double step interior, circa 1760-80
1969 March $1,175.00

Mahogany Hepplewhite secretary with blind doors, circa 1780-1800
1969 March $425.00

Cherry slant top desk with double step interior and dovetail bracket base, circa 1760-1780
1969 March $1,100.00

Chippendale maple slant top desk, circa 1760-80

1969 May $1,000.00

Hepplewhite cherry secretary with French feet, circa 1780

1969 June $1,025.00

Chippendale maple slant top desk with fine interior, circa 1760

1969 June $1,150.00

Chippendale cherry slant top desk, circa 1780

1969 June $900.00

Pine desk on frame in single unit, circa 1700

1969 September $600.00

a. Pewter whale oil lamps, American, circa 1800-20

Pair $520.00

b. Book flask, circa 1850

$230.00

c. Pewter ink well, circa 1820

$70.00

Cherry slant top desk with fluted corner columns ogee bracket base, circa 1780
1969 September $1,800.00

Fruitwood partners desk, circa 1820
1969 September $370.00

Mahogany two part bookcase, circa 1840
1969 September $800.00

Chippendale desk on ball and claw foot
frame with unique apron, circa 1760
1970 January $4,750.00

Marquetry ladies desk with ormolu trim,
circa 1860

1969 September $475.00

Curly maple slant top desk with bracket base, circa 1780

1970 February $1,025.00

Fine Chippendale mahogany serpentine-front desk with ogee bracket base and fan carving on apron, block and fan carved interior, original large Chippendale brasses, circa 1760-80

1970 March $2,000.00

Cupboards

Pine two part corner cupboard with dentil molding at top and bracket base, circa 1800
1964 September $625.00

Pine corner cupboard with clover leaf shelves and double panel door, circa 1790
1966 July $330.00

Pine cupboard, two part, with panelled doors and sides, stile feet, circa 1740
1964 September $475.00

Walnut and mahogany marquetry inlaid cupboard, circa 1760

1966 May $170.00

New England pewter cupboard with hooded top, circa 1750

1966 July $1,000.00

Formal pine corner cupboard with top cut off, circa 1750

1966 July $200.00

Pine corner cupboard with clover leaf shelves in as found condition, circa 1750
1966 July $675.00

Pine pewter dresser, circa 1720
1966 July $1,525.00

Two part grained pine cupboard, circa 1820-40

1966 August $70.00

William and Mary hanging cupboard, English, circa 1700-20

1968 August $210.00

Pine hutch cupboard with shoe feet and H hinges, circa 1770

1966 October	$225.00
a. Pewter plate	$ 90.00
b. Tea pot	$ 90.00
c. Basin	$ 60.00
d. Basin (down)	$ 50.00
e. Smooth rim plate	$135.00

Chippendale mahogany two part corner cupboard with H hinges, circa 1780

1966 August $1,025.00

Dry sink with double breadboard top, circa 1780

1968 August $150.00

*New England pine dresser, sorry no price
on contents, circa 1760*
1968 July $1,025.00

Pine pewter cupboard with rattail hinges, circa 1770-80

> 1968 August $450.00

a. Burl bowl, circa 1760

> 1968 August $115.00

Doctors cupboard, shelf folds down to writing lid, circa 1780-1800

> 1968 August $500.00

English oak pewter dresser, circa 1740

> 1968 August $150.00

Cherry two part corner cupboard with glazed doors and spoon racks, fluted pilaster, circa 1780-1800
                    1968 August $725.00

Pine corner cupboard, circa 1780
        1968 August $270.00

Oak panel wall cupboard, circa 1720-40
        1968 August $55.00

Cupboard base, American oak, circa 1680
          1969 September $650.00
a. Covered Bible box $1,025.00
b. Pair Bennington candle sticks, circa
   1850   pr. $260.00

Chippendale mahogany two drawer linen press, cupboard top and ogee bracket base, circa 1760-80
       1969 March $450.00

Pine step back cupboard
       1969 March $360.00
a. Third shelf on left mocha pitcher
                $120.00
b. Third shelf on right mocha pitcher
                $130.00
c. Bottom shelf on right squat bottle
                $140.00

Oriental teakwood curio cabinet
1969 October $700.00

Pine architectural corner cupboard with glazed doors, circa 1800
1970 February $700.00

Fruitwood Armoire, circa 1830
1969 September $925.00

Pewter

Collection of Pewter, limited number of items priced
TOP SHELF: *a. Coffee Pot* $135.00 *b. Pitcher* $200.00 *c. Miniature Queen Anne tea pot* $110.00 *d. Covered water pitcher* $170.00 *e. Coffee pot* $290.00
BOTTOM SHELF: *a. Basin* $100.00 *b. Basin* $100.00 *c. Covered sugar* $110.00 *d. Plate behind covered sugar* $80.00 *e. Spittoon* $175.00 *f. Swedish dinner pail* $95.00

1964 July

Collection of Pewter

TOP SHELF: *a.* $37.50   *b.* $14.00   *c.* $14.00   *d.* $18.00   *e.* $12.00   *f.* $12.00
g. $32.50

SECOND SHELF: *a.* $13.00   *b.* $25.00   *c.* $15.00   *d.* $15.00   *e.* $7.00   *f.* $13.00
g. $22.00

THIRD SHELF: *a.* $35.00   *b.* $35.00   *c.* $30.00   *d. pr.* $40.00   *e.* $30.00

BOTTOM SHELF: *Plates a.* $52.50   *b.* $67.50   *c.* $65.00   *d. Candlesticks* $50.00
e. Flagon $35.00   *f. Mug* $27.50

1965 November

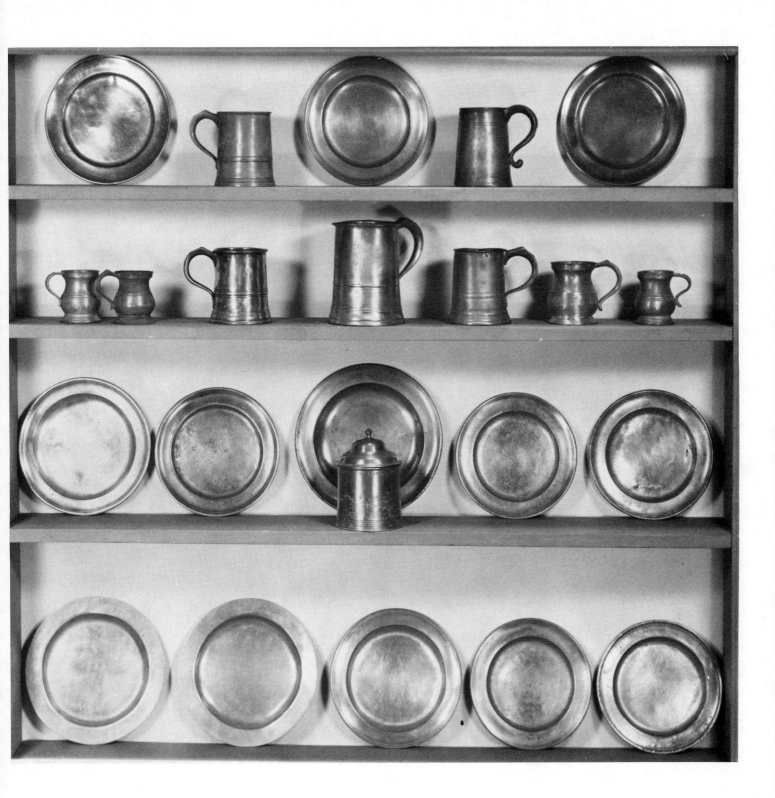

Collection of Pewter

TOP SHELF: *a.* $55.00   *b.* $30.00   *c.* $60.00   *d.* $37.50   *e.* $215.00

SECOND SHELF: *a.* 12.00   *b.* $12.00   *c.* $15.00   *d.* $35.00   *e.* $15.00   *f.* $9.00 *g.* $9.00

THIRD SHELF: *a.* $35.00   *b.* $65.00   *c.* $75.00   *d.* $55.00   *e.* $40.00   *f.* $55.00

BOTTOM SHELF: *a.* $100.00   *b.* $55.00   *c.* $40.00   *d.* $100.00   *e.* $50.00

1966 February

91

Communion set in pewter, English, circa 1740   1966 March, set $475.00

Pewter collection:

TOP SHELF: *each* $40.00

SECOND SHELF: *a.* $40.00 *b.* $40.00 *c.* $65.00 *d.* $45.00 *e.* $45.00

THIRD SHELF: *a.* $30.00 *b.* $45.00 *c.* $70.00 *d.* $90.00 *e.* $40.00 *f. Pair of lamps* $100.00

BOTTOM SHELF: *a.* $50.00 *b.* $110.00 *c.* $50.00 *a. Coffee pot* $80.00 *b. Coffee pot* $90.00

1966 September

Shelf of pewter
TOP SHELF: *Set of Pewter measures* $150.00   *Porringer* $40.00
CENTER SHELF: *Pewter plate* $120.00   *Plate* $27.50   *Plate* $27.50   *Deep Dish* $47.50   *Plate* $22.50
BOTTOM SHELF: *Tea Pot* $25.00   *Beaker* (*Danforth*) $110.00   *Inkwell* $27.50 *Candlestick* $30.00   *Pitcher* (*Homan*) $50.00   *Charger* $50.00   *Deep Dish* $50.00 *Deep Dish* $45.00

1967 March

TOP ROW: *a.* $80.00   *b.* $45.00   *c.* $32.50   *d.* $30.00
CENTER ROW: $140.00 *the set*
BOTTOM ROW: *a.* $32.50   *b.* $67.50   *c.* $40.00   *d.* $17.50   *e.* $20.00   *f.* $45.00

1968 November

TOP SHELF: *Set of Measures, set* $170.00
CENTER SHELF: *Plates a.* $200.00   *b.* $45.00   *c.* $80.00   *d.* $55.00   *e.* $42.00
Beakers a. $37.00   *b.* $45.00   *c.* $55.00   *Salt* $22.00   *Lamp* $34.00   *Beaker* $25.00
BOTTOM SHELF: *Plates a.* $90.00   *b.* $120.00   *c.* $105.00   *Ladle* $40.00   *Tea Pot*
$65.00   *Basin* $90.00   *Tea Pot* $70.00   *Porringers a.* $65.00   *b.* $70.00   *c.* $105.00
1969 June

TOP SHELF $90.00 $130.00
MIDDLE SHELF $150.00 $240.00 $90.00
BOTTOM SHELF *Plates, each* $45.00
                  Tea pot $90.00
                  Measure $22.00
                  Tea pot $65.00
                          1969 July

Pewter Porringers, circa 1780-1800
a. $170.00   *b.* $170.00   *c.* $975.00   *d.* $220.00   *e.* $240.00
Small Porringers
a. $120.00   *b.* $100.00   *c.* $140.00
Spoons a. $210.00   *b.* $100.00,   1969 September

97

Collection of Pewter

TOP SHELF: *a.-g. Mugs, pr.* $110.00 *b. Plate* $230.00 *c. Mug* $45.00 *d. Deep dish* $150.00 *e. Mug* $45.00 *f. Plate* $50.00

SECOND SHELF: *a.-k. Pair of bull's-eye lamps, each* $350.00 *b. Wooden plate* $40.00 *c. Pepper shaker* $10.00 *d. Whale oil lamp* $95.00 *e. Teapot* $125.00 *f. Whale oil lamp* $60.00 *g. Pepper shaker* $25.00 *h. Wooden plate* $25.00

THIRD SHELF: *a. Beaker* $27.00 *b. Creamer* $90.00 *c. Plate* $40.00 *d. Whale oil lamp* $65.00 *e. Coffee Pot* $110.00 *f. Sparking lamp* $70.00 *g. Plate* $30.00 *h. Tea pot* $120.00 *i. Beaker* $30.00 *j. Plate* $30.00

BOTTOM SHELF: *a.-g. Pair of candlesticks, pr.* $180.00 *b. Mug* $40.00 *c. Porringer* $85.00 *d. Tea pot* $85.00 *e. Porringer* $60.00 *f. Inkwell* $80.00

1970 January

Collection of Pewter

TOP SHELF: *a. Whale oil lamp $75.00   b. Mug $20.00   c. Mug $27.50   d. Mug $12.50   e. Whale oil lamp $75.00*

SECOND SHELF: *a. Mug $30.00   b. Two handled porringer $50.00   c. Pepper $45.00 d. Whale oil lamp $90.00   e. Rare 5⅞" diameter plate marked T. Danforth $400.00 f. Whale oil lamp $55.00   g. Porringer $50.00   h. Mug $30.00*

THIRD SHELF: *a. Mug $25.00   b. Plate $25.00   c. Beaker $10.00   d. Deep dish $55.00   e. Inkwell $60.00   f. Plate $25.00   g. Mug $50.00*

BOTTOM SHELF: *a. Tea Pot $65.00   b. Kettle lamp $60.00   c. Serving dish $55.00 d. Bull's-eye lamp, in tin $130.00   e. Coffee Pot $75.00*

1970 February

TOP SHELF: *a. Wooden scoop* $15.00   *b. Iron Porringer* $27.50   *c. Covered wooden salt* $7.50   *d. Small wooden bowl* $25.00   *e. Butter stamp* $25.00   *f. Iron Porringer* $27.50   *g. Bennington Toby* $17.50

SECOND SHELF: *a. Pewter whale oil lamp* $70.00   *b. Pewter whale oil lamp* $60.00 *c. Pewter mug* $24.00   *d. Wooden pitcher* $25.00   *e. Pewter haystack measures* $75.00, $37.00, $50.00

THIRD SHELF: *a. Chestnut bottle* $45.00   *b. Pewter pitcher* $30.00   *c. Pewter Queen Anne tea pot* $45.00   *d. Pewter spoon holder and spoons* $22.50   *e. Iron rush light* $50.00   *f. Pewter syrup* $7.50

FOURTH SHELF: *a. Pewter candlesticks, pr.* $90.00   *b. Pewter mugs* $22.00, $25.00 *c. Pewter Queen Anne plate* $17.50   *d. Pewter tea pot* $45.00

1970 March

Mirrors

One of pair of gilded mirrors, circa 1800
1964 July, pr. $700.00

Eagle convex mirror, gilded, circa 1800-20
1965 June $160.00

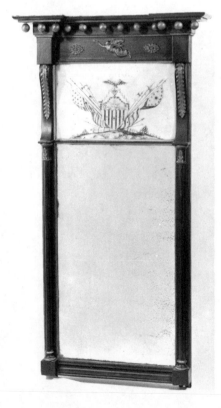

◄ *Sheraton states mirror with reverse painted*
shield and flag, circa 1820
1966 July $260.00

Queen Anne mahogany mirror with gilded
decoration, circa 1740-60 ►
1966 March $230.00

Grouping of small mirrors, circa 1700-60
a. $50.00   *b.* $45.00   *c.* $170.00
d. $25.00   1966 July

Queen Anne mahogany mirror, circa 1720
1966 August $700.00

Double size Chippendale mirror, circa 1760-80

1966 August $1,650.00

Queen Anne mirror, circa 1740
1966 October $250.00

Mahogany Chippendale mirror, circa 1780
1966 November $115.00

Courting mirror, circa 1680-1700
1967 January $130.00

Chippendale mirror with gilded eagle, circa 1750-80
1967 January $160.00

Fine Adams style gold leaf mirror with carved basket of fruit, circa 1780-1800
1967 March $350.00

Queen Anne mirror with engraved glass, circa 1740

1968 January $500.00

Queen Anne 46" two part mirror with applied gold leaf shell, circa 1740

1967 November $2,125.00

Girandole convex mirror, with candle sconce, circa 1800-20

1968 February $625.00

Convex mirror with eagle, circa 1800-20
1968 March $225.00

Sheraton picture mirror, circa 1800-10
1968 March $260.00

Queen Anne mirror, circa 1740-60
                    1968 July $500.00

Hepplewhite gold leaf mirror with baskets
of fruit, circa 1780-1800
                    1968 March $260.00

a. *Country Queen Anne mirror, circa* 1740-60,   1968 July $240.00

b. *Country William and Mary mirror, circa* 1720-40,   1968 July $65.00

c. *Courting mirror, circa* 1780-1800,   1968 July $185.00

Mahogany Queen Anne mirror, circa 1740-1760

1968 August $95.00

Chippendale mahogany mirror, 1760-80
1968 October $575.00

Sheraton gold leaf mirror, circa 1820
1968 November $110.00

Sheraton picture mirror in fine condition,
circa 1800
1969 February $160.00

Chippendale mahogany looking glass, circa 1760-80

1969 March $200.00

a. Miniature courting mirror, circa 1780-1800

1969 September $500.00

b. Queen Anne painted decoration mirror, circa 1720

1969 September $1,275.00

Gilded mirror, circa 1840
      1969 October $150.00

Chippendale mirror, 1760-80
      1969 September $375.00

Large wall mirror, circa 1850
      1969 September $100.00

Salem mirror, circa 1800-20
        1970 January $250.00

States mirror, gold leaf with cornucopia carving
        1970 January $140.00

Lighting
Devices

Bell metal chandelier, six branches, probably English, circa 1750-80
                    1965 March $650.00

Pewter chandelier, English origin, circa 1800-20

                    1965 October $210.00

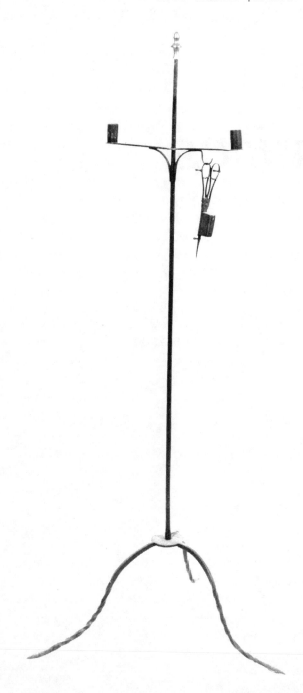

Early wrought iron standing lighting device, note brass finial and candle snuffer hook, circa 1750
                    1966 May $280.00

Brass chandelier, six branch with leaf and flower motif, probably English, circa 1780-1800

1965 November $375.00

Unusual candle lantern with four candles, circa 1780

1966 July $240.00

Collection of lighting devices
a. Pewter bull's-eye lamp $145.00   b. Sun Onion lantern $65.00   c. Pan lamp with handle $220.00   d. Table rush light $60.00   e. Wrought iron candle stick $75.00
1966 July

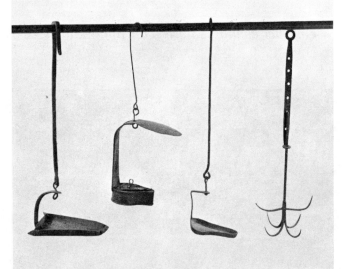

a. *Hanging pan lamp* $45.00 b. *Tin betty lamp* $150.00 c. *Hanging pan lamp* $37.50 d. *Trammel meat hook* $130.00 *circa* 1720-50 1966 June

Three forms of tin sconces, circa 1780
a. $105.00 *b.* $180.00 *c.* $70.00
1966 July

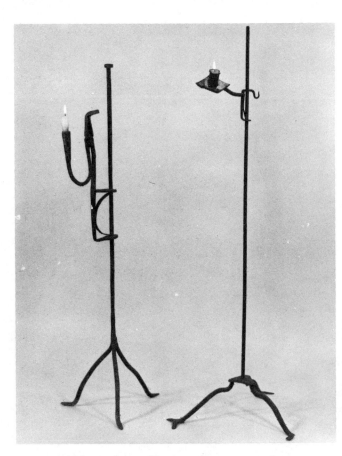

a. *Rush and candle standing wrought iron lighting device, circa 1740*
1966 July $320.00
b. *Adjustable candle lighting device, note hook for candle snuffers, circa 1740*
1966 July $350.00

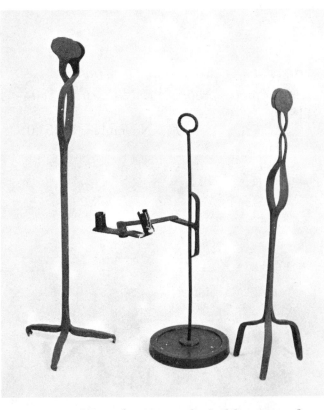

a.-c. *Lighting device for the holding of and burning of burl knots, circa 1740*
1966 July, each $80.00
b. *Table lighting device with ratchet arm for burning candles, circa 1740*
1966 July $250.00

Lamp Collection, circa 1740-80
a. Betty lamp and stand $40.00   b. Lard oil lamp, standing or hanging $30.00
c. Tin whale oil lamp with shade $70.00   d. Tin double spout whale lamp $45.00
e. Tin whale oil lamp with wick pick $45.00   f. Tin betty lamp with stand $35.00
1966 July

a. Tin tinderbox $42.50   b. Tin candle box $50.00   c. Iron van lamp $100.00
d. Flint striker $50.00   e. Stick and candle holder $50.00
f. Double tin candle lighting device $45.00
circa 1740-80   1966 July

119

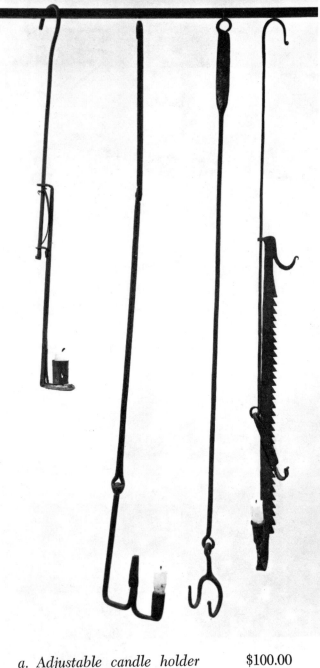

Wood and tin candle lantern, circa 1760
1966 July $55.00

a. *Adjustable candle holder* $100.00
   b. *Rush and candle holder on swale*
                                         $300.00
c. *Single chop roaster* $ 52.50
d. *Ratchet trammel candle holder* $330.00
   circa 1740-80,   1966 July

Pair of oval tin sconces, circa 1740-60
1966 August, each $160.00

120

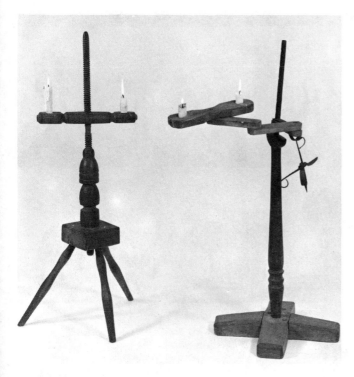

a. Screw post candle stand, circa 1720-50
                        1966 July $400.00
b. Cross base candle stand with ratchet
   arm, circa 1720-50
                        1966 July $185.00

Group of hanging lighting devices
a. $140.00   *b.* $55.00   *c.* $55.00   *d.* $100.00   *e.* $70.00   *f.* $80.00   *g.* $100.00
h. $60.00   *i.* $90.00

                                       1967 November

Whale Oil lamps, in tin, pewter, and brass
TOP SHELF: *a.* $22.50   *b.* $35.00   *c.* $22.50   *d.* $15.00   *e.* $27.50   *f.* $47.50
g. $20.00   *h.* $35.00   *i.* $40.00
SECOND SHELF: *a.* $18.00   *b.* $27.50   *c.* $20.00   *d.* $20.00   *e.* $22.00   *f.* $12.00
g. $18.00
THIRD SHELF: *a.* $85.00   *b.* $22.00   *c.* $20.00   *d.* $28.00   *e.* $27.50   *f.* $22.50
g. $17.50
BOTTOM SHELF: *a.* $25.00   *b.* $50.00   *c.* $45.00   *d.* $47.50   *e.* $55.00   *f.* $50.00
g. $65.00   *h.* $75.00

1967 November

Pair of Dresden candlesticks
1967 January each $135.00

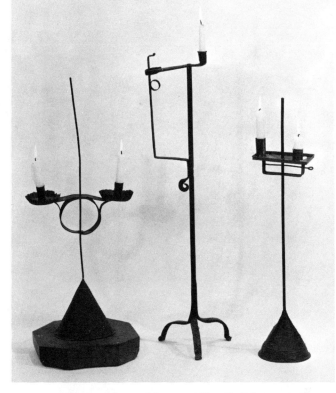

a. *Adjustable table candle holder, circa 1750-80*
1967 November $170.00
b. *Rush and candle holder, circa 1750-80*
1967 November $205.00
c. *Adjustable double tin candle holder*
1967 November $160.00

a. *Adjustable table lamp with tin burners, circa 1750-1800*
1967 November $135.00
b. *Pan lamp, for floor or table, circa 1750-1800*
1967 November $100.00
c. *Adjustable betty lamp, circa 1750-1800*
1967 November $150.00
d. *Adjustable pan lamp, circa 1750-1800*
1967 November $45.00

Candle lanterns, circa 1750
a. $50.00   b. $110.00   c. $50.00
1967 November

123

Collection of candle molds, circa 1770
a. $55.00   *b.* $165.00, *wood frame*   *c.* $22.50   *d.* $7.50   *e.* $17.50   *f.* $25.00
1967 November

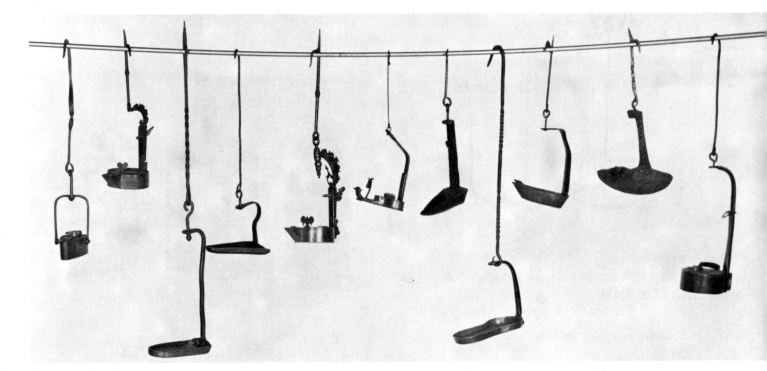

Hanging lighting devices
a. $45.00   *b.* $52.00   *c.* $60.00   *d.* $55.00   *e.* $60.00   *f.* 50.00   *g.* $40.00
h. $90.00   *i.* $42.00   *j.* $75.00   *k.* $45.00

1968 March

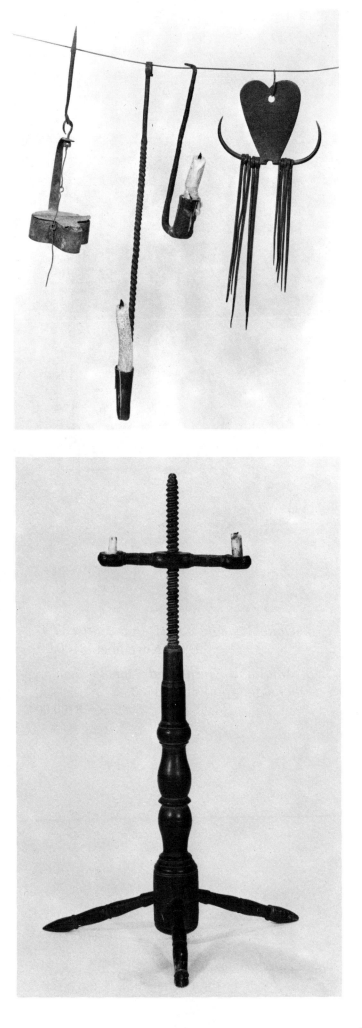

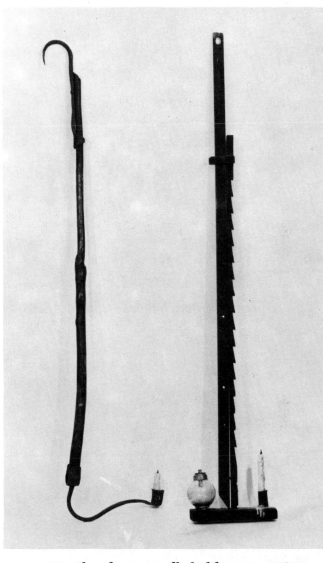

a. Betty lamp, circa 1760-80
1968 July $30.00
b. Iron candle holder, circa 1760
1968 July $150.00
c. Iron candle holder, circa 1760
1968 July $95.00
d. Skewer holder with skewers, circa 1760
1968 July $400.00

a. Wood and iron candle holder, circa 1760
1968 July $475.00
b. Rachet lighting device with peg lamp
and candle, circa 1760-80
1968 July $460.00

Screw post candle stand, circa 1760
1968 July $800.00

Four branch brass chandelier, circa 1820
1968 November $275.00

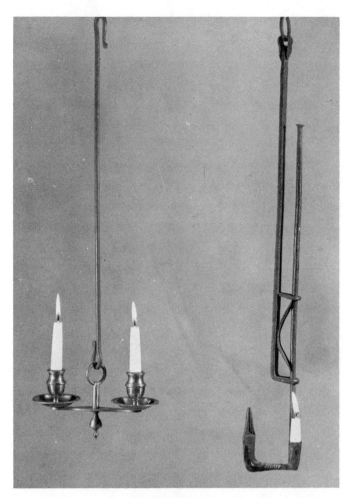

a. Double candle holder, brass, circa 1780
1968 November $100.00

b. Adjustable rush and candle holder,
wrought iron, circa 1760
1968 November $160.00

Tin chandelier, circa 1760
1968 November $300.00

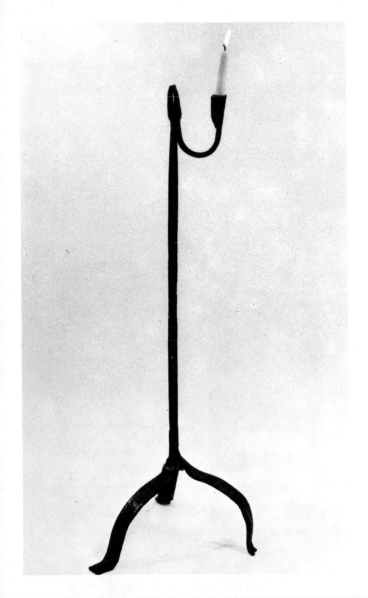

Three foot standing iron rush light and
candle holder on tripod base, circa 1770
1969 February $135.00

a. *Candle stand*	$225.00
b. *Ratchet lighting device*	$675.00
c. *Candle stand*	$500.00
d. *Rush holder*	$ 80.00
e. *Betty lamp*	$ 70.00

1969 September

Sandwich glass candlesticks in color and in pairs, circa 1850
a. pr. $210.00   b. pr. $95.00   c. pr. $35.00
(Center:) Canary Whale oil lamps, circa 1850, pr. $280.00   1969 September

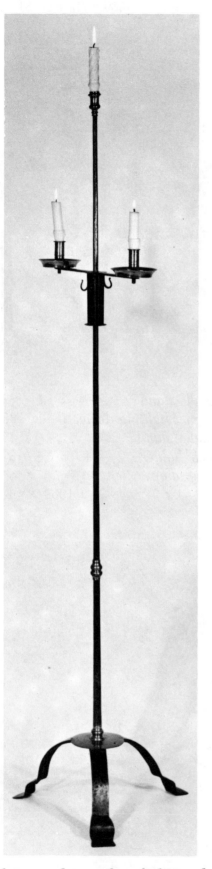

Rare brass and iron floor lighting device
1969 September $5,800.00

Candle shields 30" high, oriental gold leaf
decorated and painted paper panels
1969 October, pr. $140.00

Collection of candle molds
a. $55.00   b. $50.00   c. $30.00   d. $37.50
e. $27.50   f. $20.00, circa 1790-1800
                                    1970 March

Collection of Lanterns
a. Railroad lantern with whale oil burner
                                           $55.00
b. Candle lantern; Proctersville, Vermont
                                           $45.00
c. Pierced tin lantern $25.00
d. Candle lantern, painted tin decoration
                                           $37.50
e. Brass presentation lantern, kerosene
                                           $35.00
                                    1970 March

Fireplace Tools & Kitchen Utensils

*Three tier spoon rack dated 1729, probably
of Pennsylvania origin, circa 1729*
1964 October $825.00

*Small pine hanging shelf with scallop side,
circa* 1760

1966 July $400.00

a. *Pipe box with drawer, circa 1740-80,*   1966 July $140.00
b. *Candle box, circa 1740-80,*   1966 July $25.00
c. *Candle box, circa 1740-80,*   1966 July $80.00
d. *Pipe box with drawer, circa 1740-80,*   1966 July $260.00

a. Foot stool, circa 1780,   1966 July $75.00
b. Foot warmer with carved wood, circa 1740,   1966 July $195.00
c. Wooden piggin, circa 1780,   1966 July $35.00

Twisted wrought iron toaster, circa 1760
1966 July $90.00

a. Cabbage slicer, circa 1780
1966 July $37.50
b. Tole tea pot, circa 1780
1966 July $45.00

a. Indian mortar $45.00
b. Wooden chopping bowl with foot $85.00
c. Wooden scoop with closed handle $30.00
circa 1720-40   1966 July

133

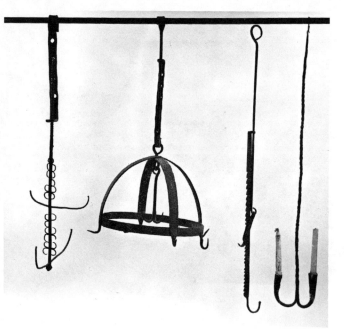

a. *Trammel meat hooks* $270.00
b. *Wrought iron meat crown* $110.00
c. *Delicate saw tooth trammel* $130.00
d. *Twisted wrought iron double candle holder* $200.00
circa 1720-50   1966 July

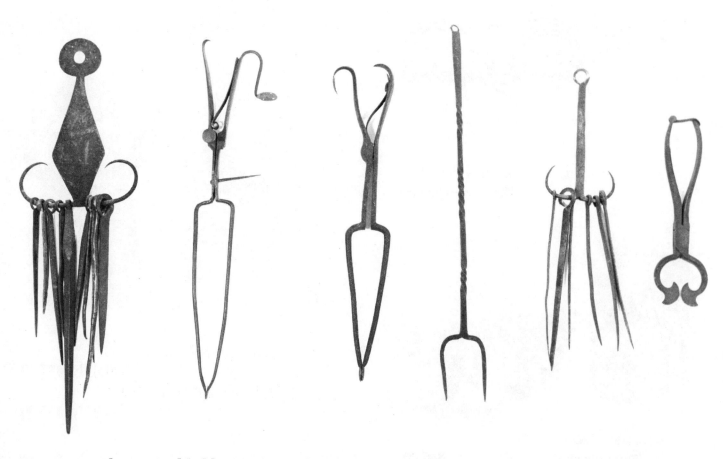

a. Skewers and holder $300.00   *b. Wrought iron pipe tongs* $270.00   *c. Wrought iron pipe tongs* $90.00   *d. Wrought iron toasting fork* $22.50   *e. Crude iron skewers and holder* $200.00   *f. Pair of iron sugar cutters* $40.00
circa 1740-80   1966 July

Pipe box with drawer and old red paint, circa 1740

1966 August $450.00

Adjustable fire screen with drawer, circa 1780   1966 August $350.00

Brass Queen Anne plate warmer, circa
1740-60   1968 March $310.00

Pine spoon rack, circa 1780
                    1968 August $90.00
a. Spoons   each $ 5.00

Spoon rack dated 1792
                1968 July $625.00

Rare pair of signed andirons by B. Edmunds, Charlestown, circa 1760-80
1969 January $450.00

Chippendale brass andirons, circa 1780
1969 February $150.00

Rosewood Captain's liquor case (complete), has brass inlay, circa 1830
1969 February $200.00

Pair of Chippendale brass andirons, circa 1760-80

1969 March $150.00

Pair of brass andirons, circa 1780
1970 January $180.00

Adam style fire grate, unusual with iron fireback, circa 1840
1969 October $325.00

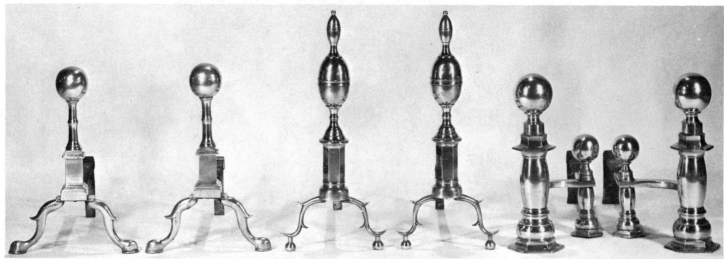

a. Pair Chippendale bell metal and brass andirons, circa 1780, $185.00
b. Double lemon top brass Chippendale andirons, circa 1780, $225.00
c. Pair signed, Hunneman, Boston, brass andirons, circa 1800, $375.00
1970 March

Weathervanes

Carvings, etc.

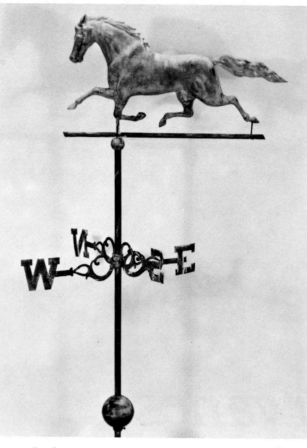

Marked J. Harris & Son of Boston full
bodied Horse, weathervane in copper
1964 September $180.00

Tin fish-monger sign, five feet long, circa
1900
1964 October $220.00

Long Island folk art wood carved scare
crow approximately 42" high, circa 1830-40
1964 October $1,050.00

Pair wood carved Indians, life size, probably not American origin, circa 1780-1800
1964 October, each $1,300.00

Carved wood cigar store Indian, circa 1820-
1840
1965 June $625.00

Carved wood eagle, circa 1760
1966 July $180.00

Excellent wood carving of Lady probably used on board ship, circa 1800
1966 July $330.00

Iron Indian (repaired), circa 1800
1966 October $425.00

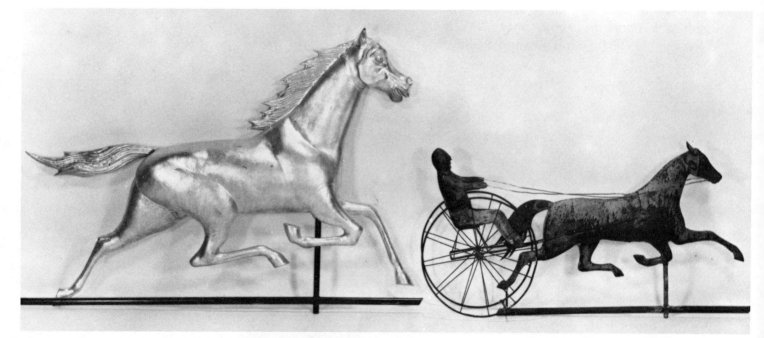

a. Swell bodied horse weathervane, circa 1820-40,   1966 October $250.00
b. Horse and sulky by L. W. Cushing and Company, Waltham, Mass., circa 1820-40
1966 October $420.00

Sheet metal weathervane, circa 1850
1968 May $60.00

Pair of five foot cast iron garden figures,
circa 1860

1968 May, pr. $220.00

143

Dolls, circa 1840
a. $110.00   *b.* $140.00   *c.* $130.00,   1968 July

Sheet metal horse weathervane, circa 1830
1968 August $70.00
a. Corn sheller, circa 1800
1968 August $55.00

Four foot, encased Clipper ship "The Rising Sun", circa 1854,   1969 May $550.00

Toy steam train, tin, steam unit complete,   1970 March $190.00

Carved wood decoys . . , each duck $60.00, each goose $110.00, 1970 March

Encased half ship model, Rosewood case, circa 1850-60, 1970 January $250.00

Sofas
&
Settees

Victorian carved sofa, circa 1800-30
1964 July $350.00

Sheraton sofa in mahogany with eight legs,
circa 1820-40
1964 July $800.00

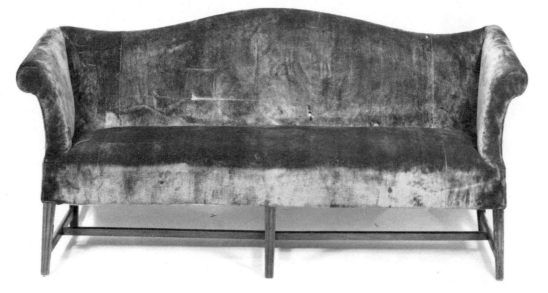

Chippendale mahogany camelback sofa
with molded legs and medial stretcher,
circa 1780
1965 August $575.00

150

Windsor settee with six legs and step down back, circa 1760-80

1965 August $420.00

Hepplewhite mahogany eight leg sofa with stretchers and molded legs, circa 1780-1800

1965 November $500.00

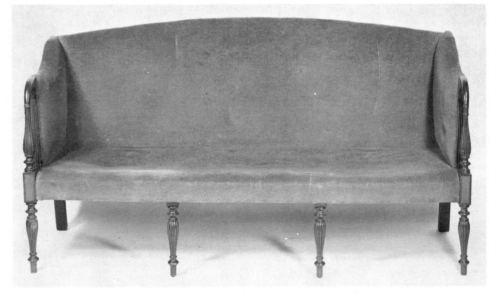

Sheraton mahogany sofa with reeded legs, circa 1820   1966 March $550.00

Marquetry settee, circa 1760
1966 May $100.00

Marquetry sofa, circa 1820
1966 May $100.00

Chippendale camelback sofa upholstered in needlepoint, circa 1750-80
1966 July $1,275.00

Settle bed, Canadian, circa 1700
1966 July $375.00

Pine form, circa 1750-60
1966 July $150.00

153

William and Mary day bed with bold turnings, circa 1680-1720

1966 July $220.00

Rare mahogany and satinwood Sheraton
sofa of finest proportions, probably Salem
— note pineapple carving and detail on
arms (in photo at upper right), circa 1800

1966 August $3,250.00

Windsor settee, circa 1780-1800
1967 March $675.00

Pine curved back settle with shoe feet, circa 1740-60

1967 March $850.00

William and Mary day bed, circa 1700-40
1967 November $425.00

Closeup of Inlaid arm, acanthus carving,
and reeded legs.

Sheraton sofa, circa 1800-20
1968 February $1,550.00

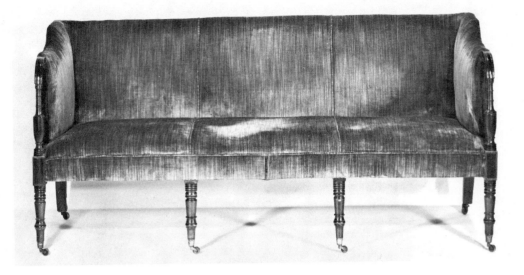

Sheraton sofa, circa 1800-20
                    1968 March $625.00

Victorian rose carved love seat, circa 1830
                    1968 April $230.00

Mahogany Sheraton eight leg sofa, circa 1800-20
                    1968 July $410.00

Windsor settee, maple, circa 1700   1968 August $200.00

Sheraton mahogany sofa with inlay, circa 1820
1969 February $375.00

Leather covered Chippendale sofa with camel back and stretcher base, circa 1760-1780
1969 March $510.00

Curly maple Duncan Phyfe cane seated settee, circa 1820

1969 June $475.00

Love seat, Fruitwood, circa 1840-60

1969 September $425.00

Sofa with two matching chairs, not shown, teakwood

1969 October, set $770.00

Queen Anne settee, English, circa 1760-80
1970 February $400.00

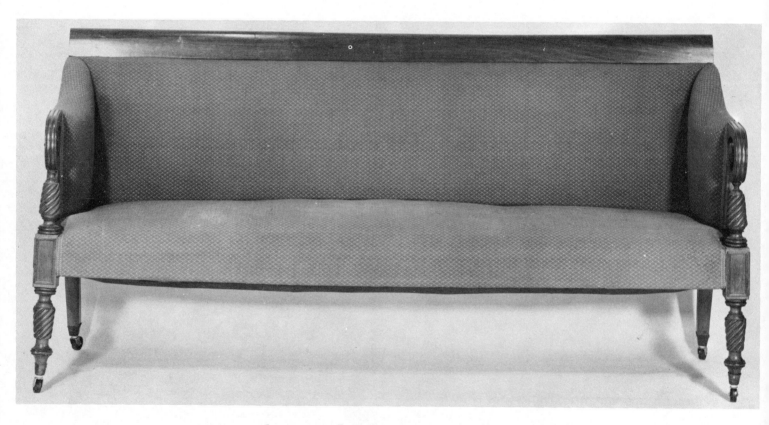

Sheraton mahogany sofa, circa 1820
1970 February $250.00

Chairs

a. Pilgrim banister back side chair with Prince of Wales crest, circa 1680-1720
1964 June $290.00

b. Oval top tavern table with splayed legs, circa 1680-1720

1964 June $280.00

c. Banister back chair with sausage-turned stretchers and with plain crest, circa 1680-1720
1964 June $155.00

a. *Bow-back Windsor rocker with comb-back, circa 1750,*   1964 June $100.00
b. *Country Queen Anne arm chair, rocker added at a later date, circa 1700-20*
                                                              1964 June $160.00

a. Queen Anne Spanish foot side chair with molded spoon back, circa 1710-30
                                                    1964 June $240.00
b. Small tavern table with shaped apron, circa 1710-30,   1964 June $290.00
c. Country Queen Anne side chair with slip seat and button feet, circa 1710-30
                                                    1964 June $230.00

Maple Queen Anne side chair with slip seat, circa 1740-60

1964 July $425.00

a. *Hoop skirt rocker with unusual slat back, circa 1760*
                    1964 July $200.00
b. *Spider leg candle stand with spade feet, circa 1780-1800*
                    1964 July $215.00

a. *Windsor tavern table, circa 1720-40,*   1964 July $400.00
b. *Comback Windsor arm chair, circa 1760,*   1964 July $220.00

a. Queen Anne Spanish foot side chair plain spoon back, circa 1720

1964 September $180.00

b. Banister back side chair with bulbous turning and shaped crest, circa 1720

1964 September $80.00

c. Yoke-back Queen Anne side chair with original button feet, circa 1720

1964 September $85.00

These chairs usually found with bulbous turnings.

a. Four-slat ladder back arm chair with mushroom arms, feet have been extended,
   circa 1700,   1964 September $110.00
b. Banister back armchair with original button feet, circa 1700
                                                        1964 September $150.00

a. *Ribbon back side chair, circa 1760,*   1964 September $80.00
b. *Country Queen Anne side chair, circa 1760,*   1964 September $85.00
c. *Country Chippendale side chair curly maple splat, circa 1760*
                                                   1964 September $75.00

*Pilgrim century carved childs chair 27"
high, circa 1700*

                 1964 October $240.00

Fan-back Windsor high chair, circa 1750-1760

1964 October $160.00

Single slat 18th century high chair with unique arms, circa 1720

1964 October $300.00

Chippendale wing chair with molded legs, circa 1750-80

1964 October $625.00

Pair Queen Anne Spanish foot side chairs with molded backs, circa 1710-30
1964 October each $290.00

Hepplewhite mahogany side chair (one of a set of six), circa 1800
1965 June each $160.00

a. Banister back armchair with double bulbous turnings, circa 1720
1965 March $250.00
b. Queen Anne Spanish foot arm chair, feet restored, circa 1720-50
1965 March $130.00

a. Queen Anne side chair, 1740-70,   1965 June $210.00
b. Queen Anne maple side chair, 1740-60,   1965 June $270.00

Pair of William and Mary side chairs with cane backs and seats, English, circa 1680-1700

1965 June each $55.00

Chippendale wing chair with medial stretcher, circa 1750-80
> 1965 August $190.00

Hepplewhite mahogany wing chair, circa 1780-1800
> 1965 October $400.00

Rare wainscot chair, circa 1700
> 1965 August $170.00

Chippendale side chairs with slip seats, circa 1750-80,   1965 October pr. $320.00

Chippendale side chairs, circa 1780
1965 November pr. $180.00

Pair of Chippendale maple side chairs, circa 1780

1966 January pr. $140.00

Carver armchair, probably English, circa
1700
           1966 January $160.00

Queen Anne maple arm chair with Spanish
feet, circa 1720
           1966 January $240.00

Double ladderback side chair, circa 1720
1966 February $105.00

Pair country Chippendale side chairs, circa
1780
           1966 March each $95.00

a. *Country Queen Anne arm chair with button feet, circa 1720*
                    1966 March $380.00
b. *Early tripod candle stand, circa 1760*
                    1966 March $160.00

Pair of Chippendale mahogany side chairs with pierced diamond shaped splats, circa 1780,   1966 May each $220.00

Pair Chippendale mahogany side chairs with pierced splats, circa 1780-1800
1966 May each $100.00

a. Banister back side chair, circa 1740,   1966 May $50.00
b. Breadboard top tavern table with splay legs and drawer, circa 1720,   1966 May $350.00
c. Chippendale side chair, circa 1750   1966 May $140.00

a. *Ladder back maple hoop skirt rocker, circa 1750,*   1966 May $125.00
b. *Splay leg tavern table with square breadboard top, circa 1740*   1966 May $120.00

Banister back rocker, fishtail crest rail, circa 1720

1966 July $135.00

177

Pair of Rhode Island continuous arm braceback Windsor arm chairs, circa 1760
1966 July each $310.00

English Queen Anne mahogany corner chair with cross stretcher, circa 1750
1966 July $325.00

Cromwellian side chair with spiral turnings, circa 1680-1700
1966 July $400.00

Carver type high chair, circa 1670-1700
1966 July $125.00

Slat back armchair with mushroom arms,
note large finials, circa 1680-1720
1966 July $500.00

Slat back weavers chair, circa 1620
1966 July $125.00

Slat back arm chair with ususual mushroom
arms, circa 1720-50
1966 July $625.00

Pair of Scandinavian side chairs, circa 1700
1966 July each $120.00

Pair early ladder back side chairs with unusual top rail, circa 1720
1966 July each $100.00

a. *Carver side chair with bold finials, circa 1680-1700,*   1966 July $280.00
b. *Carver side chair with bold finials, circa 1680-1700,*   1966 July $280.00

Carver arm chair, circa 1670-1700
1966 July $450.00

Early oxcart seat, circa 1720-50
1966 July $725.00

a. *Cromwellian side chair, note shaped stretchers, circa 1680-1720*

1966 July $250.00

b. *Cromwellian side chair, circa 1680-1720,*   1966 July $130.00

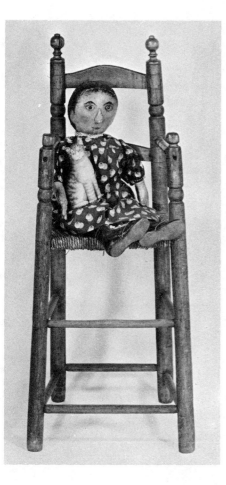

Early slat back high chair, circa 1720

1966 August $170.00

a. *Childs rag doll, circa 1820*

1966 August $90.00

*Pair banister back side chairs, note square
seat corners, circa 1720-40*
1966 August each $190.00

*Pair Spanish foot Queen Anne side chairs
with molded backs, circa 1720*
1966 August each $450.00

*Two early banister back side chairs of fine
quality, note stretchers, circa 1700-20*
1966 August each $225.00

*Pair of early banister back side chairs,
circa 1680-1700*
1966 August each $250.00

Two maple Queen Anne side chairs, circa 1740-60

1966 August a. $1,075.00
b. $ 600.00

Slat back arm chair with mushroom arms and unusual under arm turning and sausage turned front stretchers, circa 1700-20
1966 August $1,000.00

Pair of Queen Anne Spanish foot side chairs with molded back, circa 1720
1966 August each $450.00

Hepplewhite wing chair, circa 1780-1800
1966 October $515.00

Chippendale mahogany carved corner
chair with cross stretcher, circa 1780
1966 August $270.00

a. *Fan-back Windsor side chair, circa 1770,*	1966 November $65.00
b. *Splay leg one piece top table, circa 1780-1800,*	1966 November $160.00
c. *Fan-back Windsor side chair, circa 1750-70,*	1966 November $65.00

Pair of sausage turned ladder back side chairs, circa 1720
1967 January each $130.00
a. Oval top tavern table, circa 1750
1967 January $300.00

English Chippendale mahogany wing chair, circa 1750-80
1967 January $375.00

Chippendale wing chair, circa 1780
1967 March $1,000.00

Left
Comb-back Windsor arm chair, circa 1750-80,   1967 March $100.00
Center
Bow-back Windsor arm chair, circa 1750-80,   1967 March $170.00
Right
Banister back armchair, circa 1750-80,   1967 March $180.00

a. Banister back armchair, circa 1740,
                    1967 November $370.00
b. Cross base screw post candle stand,
    circa 1750-80
                    1967 November $280.00

Comb-back Windsor arm chair, circa 1770
1968 January $260.00

a. Fan-back Windsor side chair, circa 1760
1968 January $130.00
b. Fan-back Windsor side chair, circa 1760
1968 January $140.00

a. *Country Queen Anne side chair, note*
molded side stretchers, circa 1740-60
   1968 January $700.00
b. *Transitional side chair, circa 1750-80*
   1968 January $275.00

a. *Banister back side chair with fishtail*
crest, circa 1740-60
   1968 January $220.00
b. *Banister back side chair, circa 1740-60*
   1968 January $220.00

Pair Chippendale ribbon-back side chairs,
circa 1780-1800
   1968 January pr. $510.00

a., c. Pair of banister back side chairs with fishtail crests   1969 January pr. $440.00
b. Banister back armchair with fishtail crest,   1968 January $375.00

Country Queen Anne side chairs with yoke backs, circa 1760

1968 February   a. $170.00
b. $180.00

Bowback Windsor arm chair, circa 1760-80
1968 February $110.00

Sheraton mahogany wing chair, heavy legs,
circa 1800-20

1968 February $290.00

Queen Anne walnut side chairs with drake
feet, circa 1740-60
1968 February pr. $2,900.00

Mahogany corner chair with pierced splats,
Chippendale, circa 1760-80
1968 March $275.00

Banister back side chairs, circa 1740-60
1968 March each $100.00

Banister back armchair, circa 1760
1968 March $180.00

Transition side chairs, circa 1760-80
1968 March pr. $230.00

Sheraton mahogany wing chair, circa 1800-1820

1968 March $120.00

Two of a set of eight transitional dining chairs, circa 1800

1968 March set $1,120.00

Wagon seat with slat back, circa 1800
1968 April $220.00

a. *Country Queen Anne side chair*
1968 April $210.00
b. *Country Queen Anne side chair*
1968 April $310.00

Banister back armchair, circa 1760
1968 April $200.00

Mahogany Hepplewhite side chair with
shield back, circa 1780
1968 April $130.00

Queen Anne side chairs, Chinese lacquer,
set of five, circa 1760
1968 April set $680.00

Sheraton mahogany wing chair, circa 1820
1968 April $240.00

Banister back armchair with carved crest rail, circa 1760

1968 April $230.00

Slat back wagon seat, circa 1770-80
1968 July $170.00

Sheraton wing chair with mahogany legs, circa 1800-20

1968 July $550.00

Martha Washington chair, covered with green Linsey Woolsey, circa 1760-80
1968 July $1,200.00

a. *Country Queen Anne arm chair, maple, circa 1740-60,*   1968 May $140.00
b. *Banister back arm chair, maple, circa 1730-50,*   1968 May $160.00
c. *Country Queen Anne arm chair, maple, circa 1740-60,*   1968 May $140.00

Banister back armchair, circa 1740-60
1968 July $775.00
a. Candle stand with snake feet, circa
1760
1968 July $190.00
b. Capstan candlestick, circa 1720
1968 July $105.00

a., c. Carver side chairs, circa 1680-1700,   1968 July each $ 80.00
b. Carver arm chair, circa 1680-1700,   1968 July $1,025.00

a. Slat back side chair with sausage turnings, circa 1720,   1968 July $240.00
b. Slat back arm chair with sausage turnings, circa 1720,   1968 July $225.00
c. Slat back side chair with sausage turnings, circa 1720,   1968 July $240.00

Pilgrim slat back arm chair
        1968 July $450.00
a. Adjustable lighting device with small
   wooden stand, circa 1760
        1968 July $825.00

a. Carver arm chair, circa 1680-1700
                              1968 July $2,050.00
b. Candle stand, circa 1750
                              1968 July $85.00

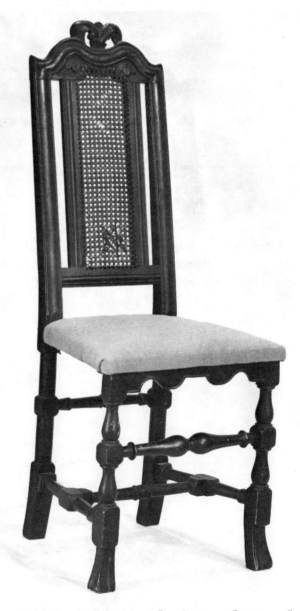

William and Mary side chair with Spanish
feet and cane back, circa 1720
                              1968 July $450.00

Country Queen Anne side chairs with Spanish feet, circa 1740
1968 July pr. $1,200.00

Set of six fancy Sheraton side chairs, newly decorated, circa 1800-20

1968 August each $55.00

Pair of maple arm chairs with Salamander slats, circa 1760

1968 August pr. $1,100.00

Pair of banister back side chairs with heart and crown crest rail, circa 1720-40
1968 July pr. $700.00

Country Queen Anne arm chair with Spanish feet, circa 1740-60
1968 August $525.00

Curly maple Empire side chairs, circa 1840
1968 August pr. $110.00

a. *Country Queen Anne side chair with button feet, circa 1750-70*
    1968 August $85.00

b. *Country Queen Anne side chair with Dutch feet, circa 1740-60*
    1968 August $180.00

Iron and wood garden bench, circa 1840
    1968 August $80.00

a. *Banister back armchair rocker, circa 1740-60*
    1968 August $70.00

b. *Ladies banister back armchair rocker, circa 1740-60*
    1968 August $120.00

Slat back oxcart seat, circa 1780
    1968 August $225.00

a., c. Pair bird cage Windsor side chairs, circa 1780,   1968 August pr. $110.00

b. Birdcage Windsor rocker, circa 1780,   1968 August $70.00

Set of six mahogany shield back side chairs,
1968 August each $175.00

Maple slat back corner chair, good turn-ings, circa 1760-80

1968 August $220.00

a. *Windsor bow-back arm chair, good turnings, circa 1760,*   1968 October $180.00
b. *Windsor high back arm chair, good turnings, circa 1760,*   1968 October $425.00
c. *Windsor bow-back arm chair, good turnings, circa 1760,*   1968 October $200.00

a. *Country Chippendale ribbon back side chair, circa 1760-80*
             1968 October $300.00
b. *Chippendale splat back side chair, circa 1760-80*
             1968 October $300.00

Comb back Windsor rocker, circa 1760
             1968 November $110.00

Banister back maple side chair with button feet, circa 1720-40

1969 January $250.00

Transitional mahogany side chair, circa 1770-90

1969 January $310.00

Maple Queen Anne corner chair, circa 1720-60

1969 January $550.00

a. Shaker rocker, circa 1800-60

1969 January $190.00

b. Shaker rocker, circa 1800-60

1969 January $290.00

a. *Shaker slat back side chair, circa 1800-1860*

> 1969 January $150.00

b. *Shaker slat back side chair, circa 1800-1860*

> 1969 January $160.00

c. *Shaker slat back side chair, circa 1800-1860*

> 1969 January $130.00

Country Queen Anne side chairs, circa 1740-60

> 1969 January pr. $900.00

Hepplewhite mahogany side chair with shield back, circa 1780-1800

> 1969 January $145.00

Maple comb-back Windsor arm chair, circa 1760

1969 January $275.00

Banister back armchair with fine proportions, note double bulbous turned stretchers, circa 1720-40

1969 January $600.00

Set of six English Chippendale side chairs, circa 1780

1969 February each $130.00

a. Cherry Chippendale side chair with transition back, circa 1780

1969 February $100.00

b. Cherry Chippendale ribbon back side chair, circa 1760

1969 February $170.00

Chippendale mahogany side chair with carved and pierced splat, circa 1780
                    1969 February $200.00

Sheraton mahogany Martha Washington chair, circa 1800-30
                    1969 February $300.00

Maple Windsor bow-back arm chair, circa 1760
                    1969 March $190.00

Pair of country Chippendale ribbon-back side chairs
                    1969 March pr. $200.00

Set of five Queen Anne side chairs with slip seats, circa 1740-60
1969 March each $575.00

Maple Queen Anne side chair with Spanish feet, circa 1740-60

1969 March $425.00

Maple country Queen Anne side chair with yoke-back, circa 1740-60

1969 March $240.00

Maple bow-back Windsor chair with writing arm and comb-back, circa 1760-80

1969 March $425.00

Slat back arm chair with mushroom arms, circa 1760

1969 March $110.00

Barrel back transition wing chair, circa
1800
                  1969 March $500.00

Hepplewhite side chair, circa 1780-1800
                  1969 May $175.00

a. Fan-back Windsor side chair, circa
1760-80
                  1969 June $60.00
b. Bow-back Windsor side chair, circa
1760-80
                  1969 June $72.50

a. Banister back maple side chair, circa
1740-60
                  1969 June $135.00
b. Country Queen Anne side chair with
yoke-back, circa 1740
                  1969 June $125.00

Banister back side chair, circa 1740
1969 September $700.00

Slat back arm chair with mushroom arms, circa 1720
1969 September $750.00

a. Maple corner chair, circa 1740-60,   1969 September $525.00
b. Windsor writing arm chair, circa 1760,   1969 September $1,175.00

Slat back arm chair, circa 1720
       1969 September $500.00

a. Tavern table, circa 1740, $475.00
b. Hanging pipe box, circa 1740, $450.00
c. Wooden pitcher, circa 1760, $200.00

a. *Tier table, circa 1860,*
b. *Victorian arm chair, circa 1820,*
c. *Bristol vase,*

1969 September $95.00
$475.00
$45.00

Pair carved Belter type chairs, circa 1840
1969 October pr. $300.00

Pair Flemish style arm chairs
1969 October pr. $300.00

a. Windsor arm chair, circa 1760,   1969 October $230.00
b. Slat back wagon seat, circa 1760,   1969 October $290.00

Teak chairs with marble insert seats
$220.00 $140.00

Comb-back Windsor arm chair with continuous arms, circa 1760-80
1970 January $320.00

Bow-back Windsor arm chair, circa 1780
1970 January $230.00

Windsor comb-back arm chair, redecorated, circa 1780

1970 February $100.00

Windsor bow-back arm chair, circa 1780
1970 February $160.00

Comb-back Windsor arm chair
1970 February $275.00

Silver

a. Pair of candelabra silver sticks with Sheffield arms by John Watson, circa 1822

1964 July, pr. $225.00

b. Fruit bowl pierced and footed by Edward Wakelin, circa 1760

1964 July $150.00

Silver coffee pot by Henry Chawner, with unusual pineapple finial, circa 1815
1964 July $450.00

a. Footed cream jug, origin Birmingham, by George Unite, circa 1820

1964 July $75.00

b. Comfit basket by Crespin Fuller, circa 1801,   1964 July $180.00
c. Slop bowl by W. M. Plummer, circa 1780,   1964 July $110.00
d. Cream jug by Andrew Fogelberg, circa 1805,   1964 July $120.00

a. *Chased chalice by Thomas Holland, circa 1815,*   1964 July $115.00
b. *Toast rack by Charles Aldrich, unusual ball and claw feet, circa 1769*
                                                      1964 July $100.00
c. *Salt and pepper by Hester Bateman, circa 1780,*   1964 July, pr. $170.00
d. *Pair of open salts with blue linings, maker unknown, circa 1830*
                                                      1964 July, pr. $80.00

Dish cross by Peter and Ann Bateman,
circa 1789

                    1964 July $375.00

a. *Plate by Paul Storrs, circa 1827-33*
                    1964 July $175.00
b. *Plate by Paul Storrs, circa 1827-33*
                    1964 July $175.00

a. *Footed salver by Hester Bateman, circa 1783,*   1964 July $700.00
b. *Pair open salts with glass linings by Hester Bateman, circa 1750*
                                                           1964 July, pr. $400.00

Tea caddy, by Peter and Ann Bateman,
unusual pineapple top, circa 1804
                    1964 July $700.00

a. *Hot water kettle and stand, by Andrew*
   Fogelberg, circa 1779
                                1964 July $625.00
b. *Coffee pot by Henry Greenway, circa*
   1779
                                1964 July $400.00

a. Pair of silver candlesticks by John Carter, circa 1768, 1964 July, pr. $575.00
b. Pierced basket with handle, circa 1766, 1964 July $350.00

a. Cream jug by Charles Hingham, circa 1806, 1964 July $130.00
b. Teapot by Duncan Urquhart & Naphtali Hart, circa 1799, 1964 July $310.00
c. Sugar bowl by Duncan Urquhart & Naphtali Hart, circa 1802, 1964 July $100.00

a. *Sauce boat by Hester Bateman, circa 1788,*   1964 July $375.00

b. *Mustard pot by Peter and Ann Bateman, circa 1796,*   1964 July $300.00

c. *Wine strainer by Hester Bateman, circa 1784,*   1964 July $100.00

d. *Cream jug by Hester Bateman, circa 1788,*   1964 July $325.00

e. *Basting spoon by Peter, Ann & William Bateman, circa 1803,* 1964 July $70.00

f. *Serving spoon by Peter, Ann & William Bateman, circa 1803,* 1964 July $40.00

g. *Pair of ladles by Hester Bateman, circa 1781,*   1964 July, pr. $190.00

h. *Pair of sugar tongs by Hester Bateman, circa 1780,*   1964 July $70.00

a. *Pair of sauce boats, Dublin, Wm. Supple, circa 1745,* 1964 July, each $275.00

b. *Cream jug, Dublin, Matthew West, circa 1769,*   1964 July $225.00

a. *Cream jug by George Smith, circa 1791,*   1964 July $100.00
b. *Footed salver by Robert Rew, circa 1767,*   1964 July $325.00
c. *Cream jug by Henry Chawner, circa 1792,*   1964 July $70.00

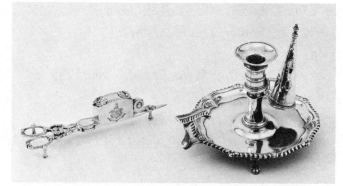

a. *Candle snuffers by Thomas Robins,*
   circa 1811
               1964 July $85.00
b. *Chamber candlestick with snuffers by*
   W. M. Cripps, circa 1759
              1964 July $140.00

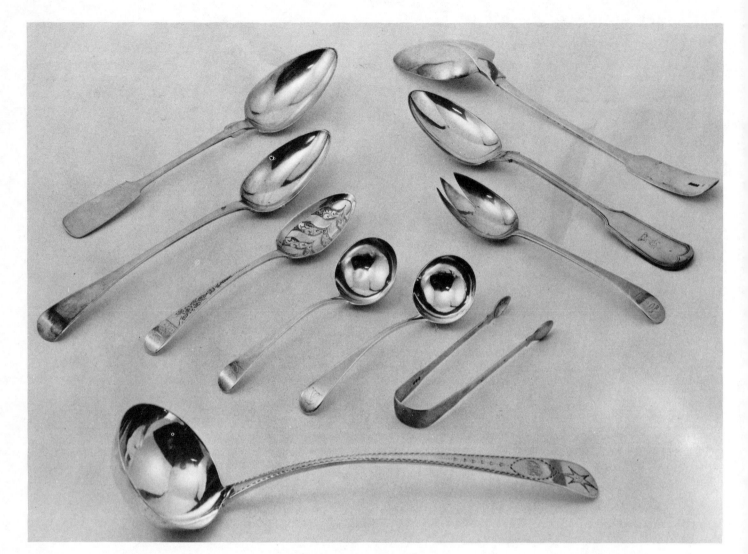

a. Serving spoon by Wm. Eley and Wm. Fearn, circa 1798, 1964 July $55.00

b. Large rattail spoon by Thomas Towman, circa 1771, 1964 July $55.00

c. Small rattail spoon, $35.00

d. Small ladle by George Smith and Wm. Fearn, circa 1788, 1964 July $35.00

e. Small ladle by Wm. Sheen, circa 1787, 1964 July $35.00

f. Tongs, $22.50

g. Large ladle, Dublin, by Samuel Purdon, circa 1801, 1964 July $100.00

Upper right: *h.* $20.00, *i.* $35.00, *j.* $35.00

a. Pair of Sheffield candelabra, circa 1724,   1964 July, pr. $250.00
b. Pierced and chased basket with handle, circa 1724,   1964 July $240.00

English Sterling and Sheffield
(*Left to right*)
a. Nutcracker $5.00   b. Grape shears $15.00   c. Nutcracker $5.00   d. Stuffing spoon
$45.00   e. Knife and spoon $15.00   f. Pair berry spoons, pr. $50.00   g. Marrow
spoon $20.00   h. Fish knife $60.00,   1969 September

Tables & Candle Stands

a. *Mahogany spider leg table with spade feet and tip top, circa 1750-80,*   1964 June $160.00

b. *Maple snake foot candle stand cut corner top, circa 1750-80,*   1964 June $120.00

c. *Mahogany snake foot tip top table with pad feet and urn turned column, circa 1750-80,*

1964 June $145.00

Mahogany tip and turn table with bird cage support, circa 1750-80

1964 June $625.00

Queen Anne mahogany drop leaf table with shaped apron, round top and cabriole legs, circa 1760

1964 June $400.00

Hepplewhite card table with shaped top and fine taper legs, circa 1780-1800

1964 June $360.00

Sheraton mahogany serpentine card table, circa 1800-20

1964 July $200.00

*Two part Sheraton mahogany banquet
table, circa 1800-20*

1964 July $475.00

*Duncan Phyfe mahogany tambour sewing
table, circa 1800*

1964 July $625.00

*Maple Queen Anne tea table with scalloped
top, circa 1740-60*

1964 July $4,100.00

Shoe foot hutch table, Hudson Valley, circa 1740-50
1964 July $650.00

Small 26" Maple Queen Anne drop leaf table with oval top, circa 1740-60
1964 July $2,500.00

Hepplewhite card table with plain string inlay, note shaped top, circa 1800
1964 September $430.00
a. Pair blue font and clamwater base sandwich glass lamps, circa 1850
1964 September, pr. $280.00
b. Liverpool pitcher with ship transfer on side and eagle on front, circa 1800
1964 September $190.00

Mahogany Sheraton server, English, circa 1800-20
1964 July $600.00

Chippendale pembroke table with serpentine top all around and drop leaves, has pierced cross stretcher and molded legs, circa 1750-80

1964 September $300.00

Country pine Hepplewhite deck top dressing table, circa 1800

1964 September $405.00

Pine trestle-foot table with two board 6' 6" top, circa 1700-30

1964 September $600.00

Oval top tea table with button feet, note splay of legs, circa 1740

1964 September $320.00

Early tripod candle stand, circa 1760
1964 October $170.00

Mahogany Hepplewhite inlaid card table,
circa 1780
1964 October $400.00
a. Engraved bell-metal candle sticks,
medial drip pans, circa 1780-1800
1964 October, pr. $240.00

Single top tavern table with stretcher base
in untouched condition, circa 1720
1964 October $1,050.00
a. Folk art rooster, polychrome wood,
circa 1830-40
1964 October $110.00

Small oak gate leg trestle foot table, Eng-
lish origin, circa 1680-1700
1964 October $400.00

Chippendale card table flower pot inlay,
figured mahogany, circa 1780
                    1964 October $400.00

Sheraton serpentine front card table, one
of a pair, circa 1800
                    1964 October $550.00
a. Pair brass Queen Anne candle sticks,
    circa 1720

                    1964 October $180.00

Hudson Valley dish top tilt table with hex
marks, circa 1720-40
                    1964 October $975.00

Drop leaf table with eagle end cut outs,
circa 1720-40
                    1964 October $500.00
a. Comb ware platter $110.00

Maple Queen Anne drop leaf table with cabriole legs, circa 1720-50
1964 October $650.00

Oval top shoe foot hutch table, in old red paint, circa 1720-50
1964 October $700.00

One board tavern-top, single drawer, table with bold turning and medial stretcher, circa 1720-50
1964 October $650.00

Unusual hour glass table, circa 1750-80
1964 October $1,975.00

Hepplewhite cherry pembroke table with shaped cross stretcher, circa 1780
1965 March $260.00

English three fold card table with two drawers, circa 1750-80
1965 June $425.00

Hepplewhite card table, mahogany, circa 1780
1965 March $360.00

Queen Anne drop leaf table with hoof feet, circa 1740-60
1965 June $330.00

Mahogany sofa table Duncan Phyfe, circa 1820

1965 June $425.00

Early gateleg table with Spanish feet, circa 1720

1965 August $200.00

Mahogany tip top table with piecrust top carved knees, circa 1750-80

1965 June $675.00

Small American 28½" Queen Anne mahogany drop leaf table, circa 1720-50

1965 August $1,600.00

Yellow decorated dressing table with deck top, circa 1820

1965 August $150.00

a. Cherry snake foot candle stand with cut corners, circa 1750-80

1965 October $165.00

b. Hepplewhite spider leg candle stand with tip top, mahogany, circa 1780-1800

1965 October $235.00

Hepplewhite mahogany inlaid card table, circa 1780

1965 August $475.00

Rhode Island Queen Anne mahogany drop leaf table, circa 1740

1965 November $925.00

Small round tavern table with drawer and stretcher base, circa 1750-70
1966 January $220.00

Chippendale mahogany swing leg dining table with claw and ball feet, circa 1750-80
1966 February $400.00

Sheraton two drawer light stand, brass pulls, reeded legs, circa 1820
1966 February $170.00

Sheraton mahogany corner wash stand, circa 1830-40
1966 February $85.00

Tavern table with H stretcher and bread-board top, circa 1750
1966 July $550.00

Hepplewhite mahogany card table with drawer, circa 1780-1800
1966 February $125.00

New Jersey Tavern table in cherry with fine shaped apron and double drawers, circa 1760
1966 July $270.00

Splay tapered leg light stand with unusual cutout apron and old graining, circa 1820
1966 July $130.00

*Early pine gateleg table with bold turned
legs, probably Scandinavian, circa 1750*
1966 July $800.00

*Shoe foot hutch table with sponge decora-
tion and drawer in base, circa 1720-50*
1966 July $900.00

*Tavern table, splayed legs and oval top,
circa 1750*
1966 July $575.00

Pine water bench, circa 1780
1966 July $350.00
a. *Saddle jug with cover* $250.00
b. *Slip ware milk pan* $45.00

Early tavern table with breadboard top, circa 1680-1700

1966 July $875.00

Great pine gate leg table with oval top, probably not American, circa 1720-50

1966 July $425.00

Mahogany Hepplewhite inlaid card table with unusual urn inlay, circa 1780

1966 July $230.00

Shoe foot trestle hutch table with breadboard top, circa 1720-50

1966 July $925.00

Oval top maple tavern table, circa 1720-50

1966 July $400.00

Pine joint stool, circa 1700
    1966 July $400.00

*Mahogany tip top table with piecrust top,
circa 1750-80*
    1966 August $625.00

*Mahogany dish top tea table with applied
shells and drake feet (not American), circa
1720-50*
    1966 August $450.00

*Oval top tea table with button feet, circa
1700*
    1966 August $925.00

Oak joint stool, English, circa 1700
1966 August $230.00

Round top tavern table with drawer, circa
1700-20

1966 August $625.00

Cross base candle stand with round top,
circa 1720

1966 August $350.00

Tavern table with H stretcher, breadboard
top, drawer missing, circa 1700-20
1966 August $725.00

Pine and maple tavern table with bread-board top and unusual stretcher, circa 1710-30

1966 August $500.00

Two part Hepplewhite dining table, un-touched condition, circa 1780-1800

1966 August $520.00

Round top tavern table, circa 1700-20

1966 August $625.00

Mahogany Sheraton card table, circa 1820

1966 August $225.00

Snake foot tip top candle stand, fine inlay on top not showing, circa 1750-70
1966 August $360.00

Small Queen Anne mahogany table, English, circa 1750
1966 November $540.00

Early pine gateleg table with breadboard top, circa 1700-20
1966 August $300.00

Maple spade foot candle stand, circa 1780-1800
1966 November $125.00

*English Queen Anne mahogany tea table
with candle slides, circa 1750*
                    1967 January $410.00
a. *Liverpool transfer bowl* $180.00
b. *Queen Anne candle sticks* $85.00

*Sheraton flaming birch dressing table, circa
1820*
                    1967 March $270.00

*Hepplewhite mahogany oval top candle
stand with splayed feet, circa 1780-1800*
          1967 January $140.00

English mahogany tip top table with bird-cage support and piecrust shaped top, note knee carving, circa 1775-90
1967 March $550.00

Mahogany Queen Anne drop leaf table, circa 1750-70
1967 November $625.00

Hepplewhite single drawer light stand with shaped top, circa 1780-1800
1967 March $150.00

Sheraton two drawer light stand with reeded legs, circa 1820
1967 March $275.00

*Pine and maple tavern table with drawer,
circa 1750-70*
>   1967 November $300.00

*Oval top tavern table with curly maple top,
circa 1740*
>   1968 January $1,425.00

*Sheraton card table with serpentine top,
circa 1820*
>   1967 November $325.00

*Hepplewhite spider leg candle stand, curly
maple top, circa 1780-1800*
>   1968 January $190.00

Mahogany drop leaf table, circa 1750-70
1968 January $725.00

Sheraton curly maple pembroke table, circa 1800-20

1968 January $450.00

Hepplewhite mahogany card table, circa 1780-1800

1968 January $525.00

Mahogany spider leg candle stand with spade feet, circa 1780-1800
1968 February $155.00

Sheraton serving table with rope turned legs, circa 1800-20
                    1968 February $600.00

Pine and maple tavern table, circa 1760
                    1968 February $420.00

Duncan Phyfe dining table with accordion slide device, circa 1820
                    1968 March $500.00

Sheraton mahogany card table with reeded legs, circa 1800-20
                    1968 February $400.00

English mahogany Hepplewhite card table, circa 1780-1800
                    1968 March $390.00

Chippendale tip top table, circa 1760-80
1968 March $325.00

Sheraton curly maple light stand, circa
1800-20

1968 March $325.00

Oval top tavern table, circa 1740-60
1968 March $500.00

Chinese lacquered gaming table with bird
cage support, circa 1780-1800
1968 March $250.00

Maple drop leaf Queen Anne table, circa 1750-70

1968 March $700.00

Mahogany Chippendale tip and turn table, birdcage support with piecrust top, circa 1760-80

1968 April $250.00

Hepplewhite candle stand, circa 1780-1800
1968 March $135.00

Cherry spider leg candle stand, circa 1780
1968 April $150.00

Hepplewhite mahogany pembroke table, circa 1800

1968 May $150.00

Chippendale mahogany drop leaf table, circa 1760-80

1968 July $825.00

Hepplewhite mahogany inlaid card table, circa 1770-1800

1968 July $475.00

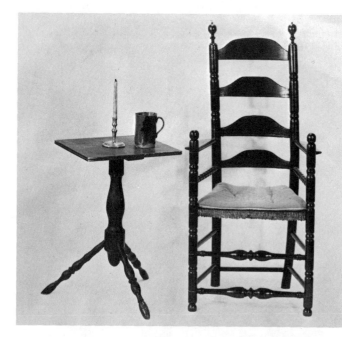

a. Primitive candle stand, circa 1760-80
1968 July $225.00

b. Slat back arm chair with mushroom arms, circa 1740-60

1968 July $375.00

Queen Anne tea table, circa 1740-60
1968 July $900.00

Small saw buck table, circa 1720-40
1968 July $500.00

Gate leg table, circa 1690-1710
1968 July $700.00

Shoe foot hutch table, circa 1700
1968 July $800.00

Windsor tavern table, circa 1750
1968 July $725.00
a. Wooden plates, circa 1740
1968 July each $30.00
b. Wooden scoop, circa 1740
1968 July $60.00

Gate leg dining table, circa 1690-1710
                    1968 July $725.00
a. Burl bowl, circa 1740
                    1968 July $200.00
b. Bell bottom candle sticks, circa 1720
                1968 July pr. $170.00

Queen Anne mahogany drop leaf table with "C" scrolls on knees, circa 1740-60
                1968 August $775.00

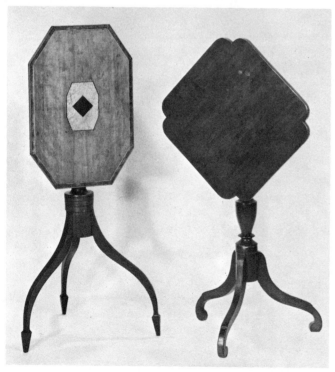

a. Cherry tip top table, inlaid, with spider legs and spade feet, circa 1780
                1968 August $180.00
b. Mahogany tip top table with cut corners, circa 1800
                1968 August $150.00

Sheraton mahogany card table serpentine top, circa 1800-20
                1968 August $140.00

Mahogany tip top table with bird cage support and dish top, circa 1740-60
1968 August $985.00

Late Sheraton curly maple serving table, circa 1830-40
1968 August $160.00

Pine sawbuck table, top not original, circa 1780
1968 August $120.00

Small maple chair table, circa 1760
1968 August $200.00

Hepplewhite country card table, birdseye maple and cherry, circa 1780-1800
1968 August $180.00

Queen Anne maple drop leaf table, circa 1740-60

1968 August $1,050.00

Gateleg table with double gate in back and single gate in front, circa 1780

1968 August $450.00

Cherry pembroke table with bowed stretcher and drawer, circa 1760-80

1968 August $450.00

Pine breadboard top table with tapered legs and drawer, circa 1790

1968 August $160.00

a. Back Row
Candle mold	$ 35.00
Skating lamp	$ 32.50
Decorated crock made in South Woodstock, Vermont	$170.00
Wooden canteen	$ 27.00
Blown mug	$ 12.50

b. Front Row
Mocha mug	$ 15.00
Brass powder flask	$ 15.00
Betty lamp	$ 27.50
Schrimshaw tooth	$ 50.00

Sheraton mahogany drop leaf table with drawer, circa 1800-20
1968 August $375.00

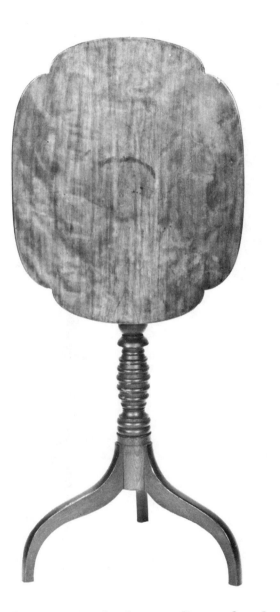

Mahogany Hepplewhite candle stand with shaped top, circa 1780-1800
1968 August $170.00

Duncan Phyfe lyre base card table, circa 1820
1968 August $235.00

a. *Mahogany spider leg candle stand, circa 1780,*   1968 October $300.00
b. *Cherry oval tip top table with spider legs, circa 1780,*   1968 October $425.00
c. *Cherry candle stand with spider legs and spaded feet, circa 1780,*   1968 October $425.00

Hepplewhite mahogany card table with curly maple inlay, circa 1780
1968 October $900.00

Hepplewhite mahogany inlaid light stand with arched cross stretchers, circa 1770-80
1968 October $1,500.00

Hepplewhite mahogany card table with inlay, circa 1780
1968 October $900.00

Hepplewhite cherry inlaid light stand with shaped top, and heart and string inlay, circa 1780
1968 October $525.00

Shaker bed side table with medial shelf, circa 1800-60

1969 January $475.00

Mahogany round card table, Hepplewhite, circa 1780-1800

1968 November $300.00

Cherry snake foot candle stand, circa 1760
1968 November $100.00

Queen Anne maple drop leaf table, cut corners and cabriole legs, circa 1740-60
1968 November $600.00

Cherry shaker table with single drop leaf and one drawer, circa 1800-60
                    1969 January $500.00

Maple Queen Anne dining table, circa 1740-60
                    1969 January $900.00

Pair Hepplewhite mahogany inlaid card tables, tops restored, circa 1780-1800
                    1969 January pr. $800.00

Cherry Shaker table, one drop leaf and two drawers, circa 1800-60
1966 January $1,550.00

Shaker single drawer table, circa 1800-60
1969 January $400.00

Two part cherry Sheraton dining table, circa 1800-20

1969 January $875.00

Maple candle stand with spider legs and shaped top, circa 1780-1800
1969 January $165.00

Mahogany snake foot candle stand, circa 1760

1969 February $155.00

Hepplewhite mahogany inlaid card table with "D" shaped top, circa 1780-1800
1969 February $525.00

Chippendale mahogany tripod table, dish top and birdcage support, circa 1780
1969 February $800.00

Mahogany pembroke table with drawer, circa 1780-1800
1969 February $325.00

English Queen Anne drop leaf mahogany table, circa 1740-60
1969 February $375.00

Sheraton mahogany table with sewing bag, circa 1820
1969 February $90.00

English Queen Anne mahogany gaming table, circa 1760
1969 February $275.00

Country pine half round table with shaped apron, circa 1780-1800
1969 March $180.00

Maple Queen Anne drop leaf dining table with straight legs and straight apron, circa 1760
1969 March $550.00

Mahogany snake foot tip top table, circa 1760
1969 March $425.00

Cherry Sheraton country card table, circa 1800-20
1969 March $250.00

Maple snake foot table, circa 1760
1969 May $200.00

Cherry snake foot candle stand, circa 1760-1780
1969 May $85.00

Maple chair table, circa 1760-80
1969 May $250.00

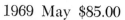

Cherry drop leaf table with shaped top, circa 1760-80
1969 June $160.00

Queen Anne maple drop leaf table with round top and straight legs, circa 1760
1969 June $430.00

Oak gate leg table with drawer, circa 1740-1760

1969 June $160.00

Maple candle stand with tip top and spider legs, circa 1780
1969 June $300.00

Cherry candle stand, circa 1760-80
1969 June $190.00

Trestle table, circa 1680-1700
          1969 September $3,700.00
  a. Burl bowl, circa 1720 $550.00
  b. Ladle, circa 1740 $ 70.00

Banister back side chairs, circa 1740-60
          1969 September each $240.00
  a. Tavern table, circa 1700-20
                                $1,150.00
  b. Shaving box, circa 1780
                                $200.00
  c. Hanging pipe box with drawer, circa
     1740
                                $625.00

Butterfly table, circa 1700-20

1969 September $525.00

a. Burl bowl $350.00

b. Scoop $120.00

Hepplewhite card table, circa 1780-1800

1969 September $475.00

Queen Anne drop leaf table, circa 1760

1969 September $875.00

Maple gate leg table, circa 1700-20

1969 September $525.00

a. Bennington candle sticks, circa 1850

pr. $270.00

b. Bennington bowl, circa 1850

$110.00

Candle stands   1969 September
a. *Tip top with spider legs, circa 1780-1800*

                   $325.00

b. *Snake foot candle stand, circa 1760*
                   $190.00

c. *Tip top table with spider legs and spade feet, circa 1780*

                   $400.00

Sheraton mahogany drop leaf table, circa 1820

1969 September $350.00

Gaming table in fruitwood, circa 1840
1969 September $375.00

Regency card table with fluted legs
1969 September $230.00

Card table, bamboo turned legs, circa 1840
1969 September $140.00
a. Oriental charger $110.00

a. *English oak side table, circa 1760*
1969 October $95.00
b. *English side chair, circa 1680*
1969 October $22.50
c. *English oak gate leg table, circa 1740-60*
1969 October $150.00

Mahogany Sheraton drop leaf table with
rope turned legs, circa 1820-40
1969 October $220.00

English mahogany Queen Anne drop leaf
table with six legs, circa 1760
1970 January $450.00

Side table in mahogany with marquetry
inlay
1969 October $275.00
a. Pair brass candle sticks   pr. $22.50
b. Oriental figurine $32.50

Queen Anne dish top tea table with unique
candle slides, note finely scrolled apron,
circa 1740-60
1970 January $5,000.00

Hepplewhite mahogany round card table with bell flower inlay, circa 1780
1970 January $525.00

Mahogany spider leg candle stand, circa 1780
1970 January $200.00

Curly maple button foot country tea table, circa 1760
1970 January $450.00

Cherry pembroke table with drawer, circa 1800
1970 February $275.00

*Mahogany tip top table with snake feet,
circa 1780*
1970 February $185.00

*Mahogany English Queen Anne table,
circa 1760*
1970 February $275.00

*Unusual candle stand with original red,
yellow and blue paint, possibly Spanish,
circa 1800*
1970 February $60.00

*Hepplewhite mahogany card table, circa
1780-1800*
1970 February $260.00

Hepplewhite mahogany inlaid card table, circa 1790-1800

1970 March $475.00

a. *Hepplewhite birch candle stand with spider legs and spade feet, circa 1790-1800*

1970 March $220.00

b. *Cherry tip top table with serpentine top and snake feet, circa 1760-80*
1970 March $300.00

c. *Duncan Phyfe mahogany tip top candle stand, circa 1800-20*

1970 March $150.00

Clocks

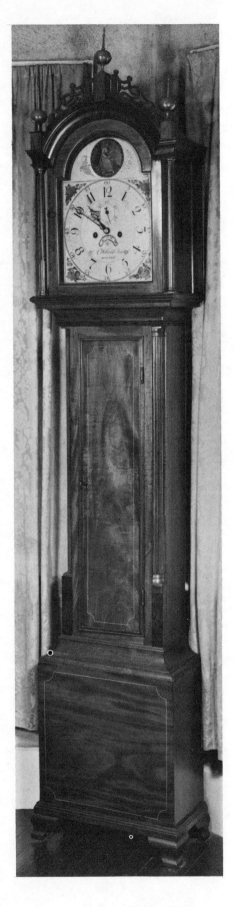

Rare mahogany grandfather clock with marked face and original 'Aaron Willard, Junior' label, circa 1820

1964 June $2,100.00

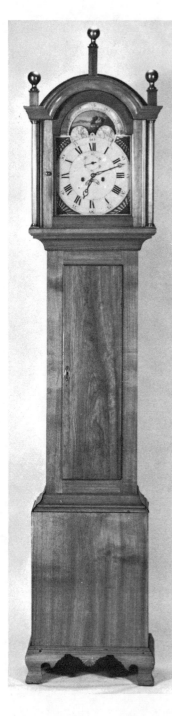

*Timothy Chandler birch grand-
father clock (mark impressed on
saddle) fret work missing, ogee
bracket base and small carving on
apron, circa 1820*

1964 September $775.00

*Fine Massachusetts shelf clock by S. Taber,
mahogany with satin wood inlay, circa
1830*

1964 July $1,850.00

Cherry case grandfather clock with quarter columns and ogee bracket base, brass works, finials missing, circa 1780
1964 September $500.00

Mahogany inlaid grandfather clock, attributed to James Cole, Rochester, New Hampshire, circa 1812
1965 June $1,000.00

Unusual pine case grandfather clock with brass dial, circa 1753
1965 March $370.00

Flaming birch grandfather clock by Benjamin Morrill, Boscawen, New Hampshire, circa 1810-20
1965 June $700.00

Rare maple grandfather clock with brass works by Jonathan Ward, Fryeburg, Maine. (Apprentice to Timothy Chandler), circa 1790
1965 August $800.00

New Hampshire maple inlay grandfather clock made in Sanbornton, New Hampshire by Elisha Smith, Jr., has gallery top, circa 1800
1965 October $750.00

Small curly maple grandfather clock with eight day movement by Philip Brown 1815, Hopkinton, New Hampshire, circa 1800
1965 November $425.00

New Hampshire mirror clock with rare eight day brass movement, by A. Chandler, Concord, New Hampshire, circa 1820
1965 November $325.00

Fine mahogany inlaid grandfather clock by A. Stowell, Worcester, with ogee bracket feet, circa 1800-20
1966 January $500.00

*Fancy gold leaf girandole clock, copy of
an original, circa 1880*
                    1966 January $425.00

Rare Connecticut acorn clock, circa 1845
                    1966 January $600.00

33" Massachusetts shelf clock untouched condition, circa 1790
1966 February $800.00

Maple grandfather clock with fluted corner columns and brass movement, circa 1810
1966 February $235.00

Pillar and scroll shelf clock by Seth Thomas, circa 1830

1966 March $340.00

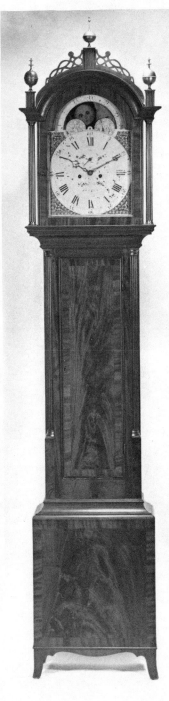

Mahogany veneer grandfather clock, by Aaron Willard, circa 1800

1966 March $2,400.00

289

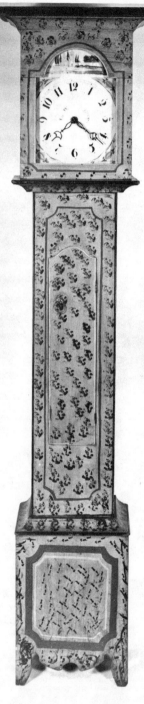

Fine New England cherry grand-father clock with fluted corner columns and brass movement, circa 1800

> 1966 May $425.00

Grandfather clock with sponge decoration by Levi Lewis, wooden works, circa 1809-23

> 1966 July $450.00

Banjo clock with gold front, circa 1800-20

> 1966 July $310.00

Banjo clock with gilded bracket,
circa 1800-20

1966 August $300.00

*English grandfather clock with
brass works, Chinese lacquered
case, circa 1760*

1966 August $375.00

*Maple grandfather clock with fruit-
wood top, made by T. Chandler and
stamped on saddleboard, circa 1820*

1966 August $1,350.00

Pillar and Scroll shelf clock made by Eli Terry, Jr., circa 1830
1967 March $425.00

Mahogany inlaid grandfather clock probably New York State, circa 1790-1810
1967 January $400.00

Mahogany grandfather clock by Nathaniel Mulliken, circa 1780
1967 March $850.00

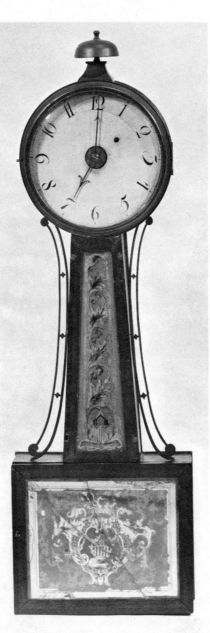

*Banjo clock with alarm bell, circa
1820*
          1967 November $700.00

*Banjo clock with gold front, marked
Aaron Willard, Jr. stamped on
movement behind dial, circa 1825
          1967 March $975.00*

*Chinese lacquered case grandfather
clock, brass works, circa 1760
          1968 January $450.00*

Banjo clock by Simon Willard and Sons, mahogany front, wood bezel, circa 1830
1968 February $550.00

Pillar and scroll shelf clock by Mark Levenworth & Co., circa 1830
1968 February $485.00

N. E. Cherry grandfather clock with brass works, circa 1820
        1968 February $825.00

Pine case grandfather clock by R. Whiting, circa 1830
        1968 March $250.00

Pillar and scroll shelf clock by Silas Hoadley, circa 1830
        1968 March $475.00

Mahogany front banjo clock with bracket, circa 1830

1968 May $200.00

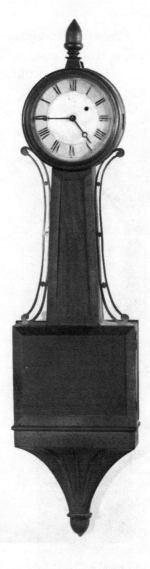

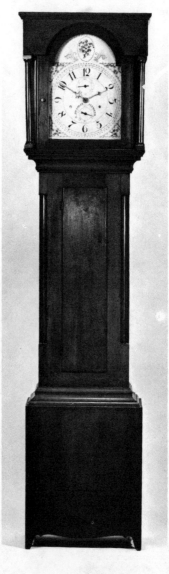

Pine grandfather clock, signed S. Hoadley, circa 1830

1968 April $250.00

Banjo clock with mahogany front and wood bezel, circa 1830

1968 April $250.00

Mahogany front banjo clock with wood side arms, circa 1830
1968 May $230.00

Pillar and scroll shelf clock by Ephraim Downes, circa 1830
1968 May $450.00

Reeded quarter columns grandfather clock by David Wood, circa 1820
1968 May $1,550.00

Clocks, circa 1830,   1968 July
a. Double decker, carved eagle with reverse painting of Washington on glass

$290.00
b. Pillar and scroll shelf clock by Eli and Samuel Terry $600.00
c. Double decker by Daniel Pratt $150.00

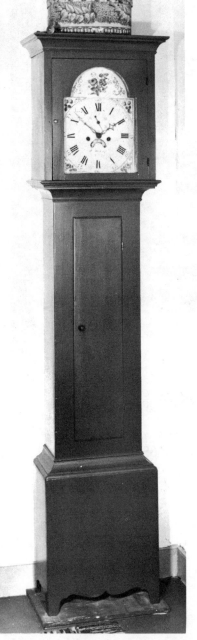

English, pine grandfather clock,
circa 1800-20
  1968 August $210.00

Pine case grandfather clock by John
Hockins, circa 1830
  1968 August $275.00

a. Hat box, circa 1830

Mahogany grandfather clock with
brass works, circa 1800-20
  1968 August $625.00

a. Massachusetts type pillar and scroll clock by Eli Terry and Sons, circa 1830,
                                                                1968 August $225.00
b. Jerome Darrow's transition shelf clock with fruit carvings and pineapple finials,
circa 1830,   1968 August $275.00

a. *Howard style banjo clock, circa 1850,*   1968 October $230.00
b. *Gold front banjo clock, circa 1820,*   1968 October $1,050.00
c. *Mahogany front banjo clock, circa 1830,*   1968 October $275.00
d. *Howard style banjo clock, circa 1850,*   1968 October $375.00

Pillar and Scroll shelf clock by Eli Terry
and Sons, circa 1830-40
1968 October $725.00

Cherry grandmothers clock, 50"
high with brass dial, circa 1810-30
1968 October $3,600.00

Cherry grandfather clock, fluted
quarter columns, with rare double
scrolled ogee bracket base, made by
Stephen Hasham, circa 1780
1968 October $3,100.00

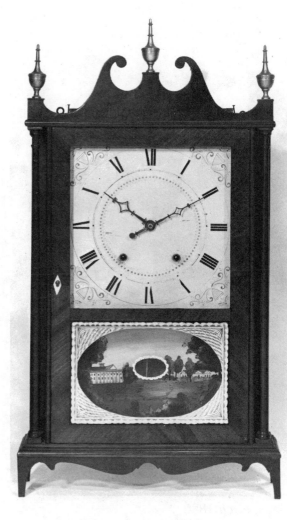

*Pillar and Scroll shelf clock by Eli
and Samuel Terry, circa 1830*
1968 November $760.00

*Transition clock by Sylvester Clarke, circa
1830*

1968 November $375.00

a. *Pillar and scroll shelf clock by Eli Terry and Sons, circa* 1830

1969 January $550.00

b. *Carved column shelf clock by Atkins Downs, circa* 1830

1969 January $70.00

c. *Transition clock by Eli Terry, Jr., circa* 1830   1969 January $250.00

Mahogany grandfather clock by Alvin Lawrence, Lowell, Massachusetts, circa 1830
1969 January $800.00

Willard type gold front banjo clock painted with ship battle and American shield on glass, circa 1830
1969 February $450.00

Mahogany lyre banjo clock, circa 1830
1969 January $750.00

a. Pillar and scroll clock by Seth Thomas, circa 1830,

1969 February $475.00

b. Transition clock with paw feet by E. and G. W. Bartholomew, circa 1830

1969 February $125.00

Acorn clock, side arms missing, circa 1830

1969 March $975.00

a. Pillar and scroll shelf clock with Atkins stamped on movement, Mt. Vernon painted on glass, circa 1830   1969 March $450.00

b. Transition clock by Riley Whiting, circa 1830,   1969 March $225.00

Mahogany banjo clock with bracket, circa 1830
        1969 March $350.00

Mahogany banjo clock with mahogany side arms, circa 1830-40
        1969 May $260.00

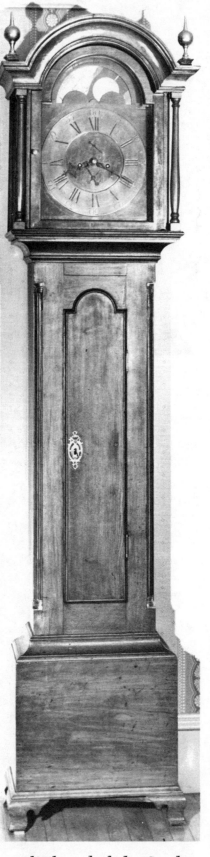

Brass dial grandfather clock by Stephen Hasham, circa 1780
        1969 September $3,100.00

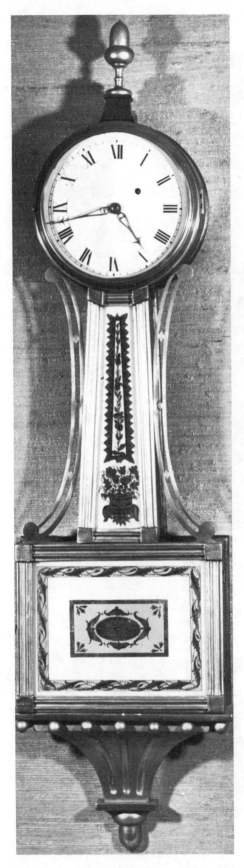

Banjo clock, circa 1820-40
1969 September $800.00

Scottish grandfather clock, circa 1780
1969 October $275.00

Fine Massachusetts shelf clock by Aaron Willard, has dish dial and painted glass in top and bottom, circa 1810
     1970 January $2,900.00

Triple decker shelf clock with hollow columns, weights run down thru the columns, circa 1840

1970 January $150.00

Pillar and scroll shelf clock by Jeromes & Darrow, circa 1820-30

1970 January $475.00

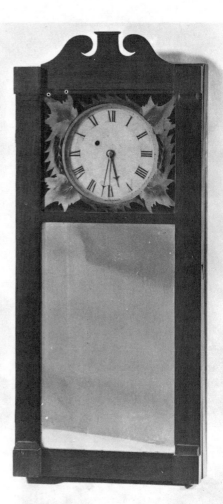

New Hampshire mirror clock, circa 1830
1970 February $350.00

Grandfather clock with brass dial,
circa 1800

1970 February $460.00

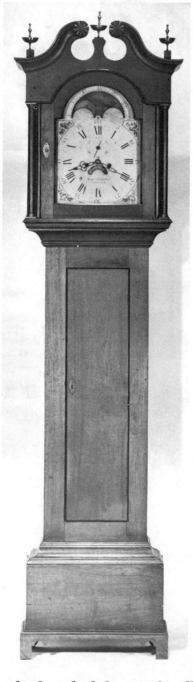

Grandfather clock by T. Chandler,
Concord, N.H., cup finials, circa
1820-30

1970 March $1,800.00

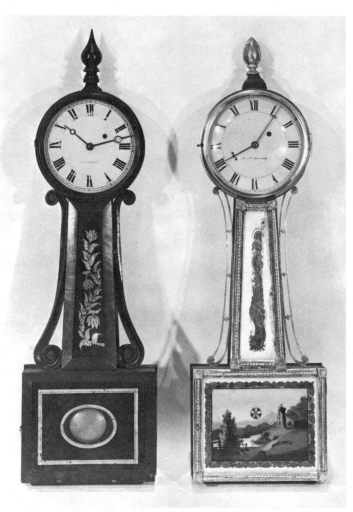

a. *Mahogany front banjo clock by W. Goodwin, circa 1830*

        1970 March $375.00

b. *Gold front banjo clock by J. N. Dunning, circa 1820*

        1970 March $825.00

Mahogany grandfather clock by John Wilkie, Scotland, circa 1820

1970 March $425.00

Beds

Sheraton field bed with reeded foot posts and square head posts, circa 1800
1964 June $600.00

Sheraton canopy top birch bed, circa 1820
1967 November $450.00
a. Appliqued quilt, sunburst pattern
$100.00

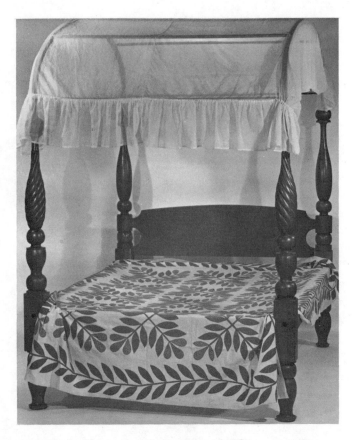

Birch Sheraton canopy top bed, circa 1820
1967 January $320.00

Mahogany Sheraton canopy bed with heavy posts, circa 1800-20
1968 March $375.00
a. Appliqued quilt
$80.00

Sheraton birch canopy top bed, heavy posts, circa 1820

                   1968 April $380.00

Coverlet, in chintz $145.00

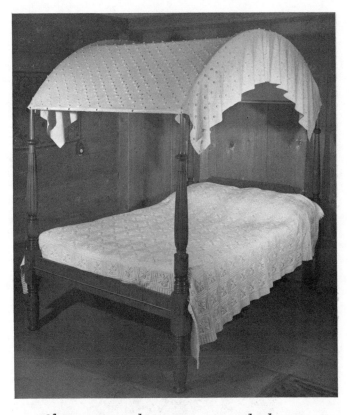

Sheraton maple canopy top bed, circa 1800-20

              1968 October $650.00

Birch, canopy top bed, circa 1800-20

             1968 May $275.00

a. Appliqued quilt, circa 1800-20

             1968 May $40.00

Sheraton canopy top bed, heavy posts, circa 1800-20

             1969 January $300.00

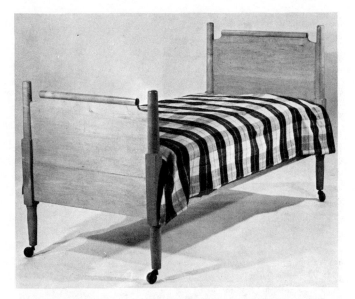

Shaker bed on rollers, circa 1800-60
1969 January $275.00

Decorative bed headboard, circa 1840-60
1969 September $65.00

Sheraton birch canopy top bed, circa 1800
1970 January $380.00

Sheraton cherry canopy top bed, circa
1800-20
1969 May $650.00

Sheraton maple canopy top bed, circa 1820
1969 May $160.00

Paintings & Prints

a. Painting on velvet, circa 1860-80,   1964 July $185.00
b. Painting on velvet, circa 1860-80, $185.00

a. Portrait of English Boy and his dog, circa 1780,   1964 July $500.00
b. Portrait of English Girl holding a flower, circa 1780, $500.00

Currier and Ives "Cares of a Family", circa 1860

1964 July $725.00

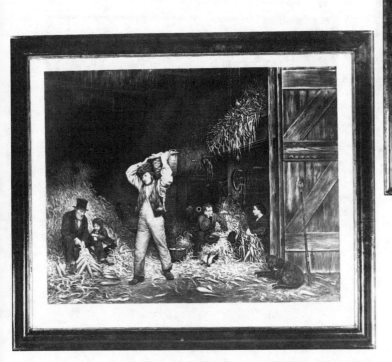

Currier and Ives "Husking", circa 1860
1964 July $600.00

Pair of Prior Type portraits, circa 1820,   1964 July pr. $900.00
Courting mirror, circa 1780-1800, $275.00

Rare Currier and Ives, large folio "Home to Thanksgiving", circa 1860
1964 July $3,750.00

Primitive landscape painting, artist unknown, circa 1800
1964 September $170.00

Pair of New England primitive ancestral portraits of man and wife, with grained frames, circa 1830,
1964 September $380.00

*Metford signed full length silhouette, circa
1850*

1964 September $40.00

*Primitive painting, artist unknown, circa
1800*

1964 October $1,200.00

*Rare N. Currier large folio "Camping Out,
Some of the Right Sort"*

1964 September $240.00

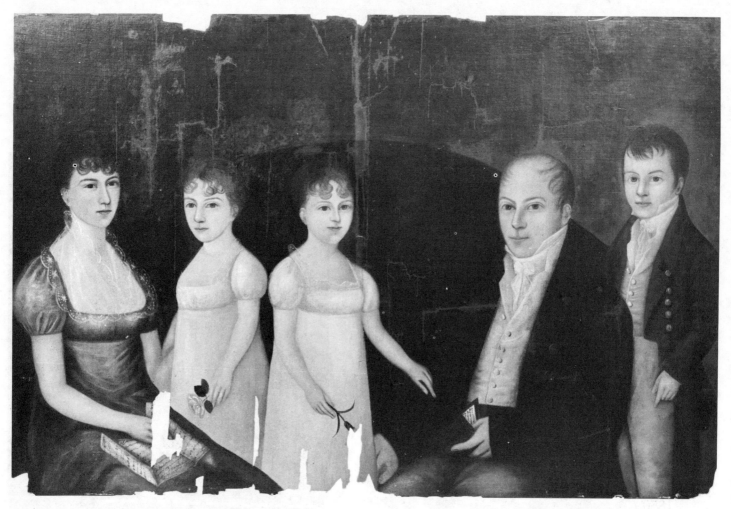

Family painting attributed to Negro artist, Joshua Johnson, circa 1800
1964 October $2,200.00

Pair primitive animal paintings, circa 1800
1964 October each $300.00

Painting of Indians, unknown artist, circa 1830

1965 June $140.00

Painting of Abigail Evans Osgood, Concord, New Hampshire, signed John Brewster and dated April 16, 1823

1965 August $500.00

Pair of portraits of Deacon Henry C. Buswell and Elizabeth Osgood Buswell, attributed to Cole, circa 1800,

1965 August each $425.00

Primitive 18th century portrait of Catalina Van Duesen holding roses, artist unknown, circa 1720-50

1965 August $2,300.00

Pair of ancestral portraits painted by Joseph G. Cole, Dover, New Hampshire, signed and dated, circa 1800,   1965 August each $100.00

Painting of gentleman, circa 1800
1965 October $220.00

Primitive painting of Mehitabel Chloe Buswell, mother of Deacon Buswell, circa 1800
1965 August $425.00

Painting of woman, circa 1820
1965 October $80.00

Painting of child, by name of Warren, from Troy, New York, circa 1800-20
1965 October $420.00

Portrait of girl holding roses with cat, circa 1800-30
1965 October $225.00

Painting of girl with dog, circa 1800-20
1965 October $250.00

Full length painting of boy with cart and whip, by an unknown artist, circa 1780-1810

1965 October $425.00

Ancestral portraits by Zedekiah Belknap, 1781, *Weathersfield, Vermont*

1965 October pr. $700.00

Paintings attributed to Prior, circa 1825-70,   1966 January a. $65.00
b. $65.00

Stumpwork scene, circa 1700
1966 March $210.00

Excellent portrait of young man, circa 1790
1966 January $250.00

Painting of lady, circa 1840
1966 May $60.00

Still life painting, artist unknown, circa 1820
1966 May $290.00

*Painting of young gentleman, signed H.
Bundy, Claremont, N. H.* 1846
1966 May $300.00

Painting of studious young man, circa 1810
1966 July $155.00

Full length painting of brother and sister, circa 1820

1966 July $610.00

Painting of Richard Gridley, circa 1730-40
1966 July $300.00

Profile painting of gentleman, circa 1790
1966 July $155.00

Still life painting, circa 1850
1966 July $450.00

Painting of girl with pet rabbit, circa 1790
1966 July $400.00

Painting of young lady holding flowers,
circa 1800

1966 July $280.00

Vermont landscape by G. G. Hole, circa 1876

1966 July $320.00

Painting of boy with dog, circa 1800-20

1966 July $260.00

Primitive painting of horse and farm yard, circa 1850

1966 July $280.00

Painting on Velvet, circa 1820-50

1966 July $80.00

Jamaica Pond, W. Roxbury, Mass., print, circa 1840

1966 July $410.00

Painting of young girl holding two cats, circa 1800-20

1966 July $370.00

Pair of portraits attributed to Prior, circa 1825-70, 1966 July each $210.00

*Painting on academy board, attributed to
Prior, circa 1825-70*
1966 July $300.00

*Painting of woman attributed to Prior, circa
1825-70*
1966 July $300.00

*Picture of sailor, painted by a Maine artist,
E. E. Finch, circa 1800-20*
1966 July $440.00

Portrait of woman, circa 1820
1966 July $500.00

Portrait of gentleman, circa 1825-50
1966 July $440.00

Portrait of grandmother, circa 1800
1966 July $325.00

*Painting of a Massachusetts coastal town,
circa 1700-20*
1966 July $325.00

Oval portrait of gentleman, circa 1720
1966 August $200.00

Painting of sisters, circa 1880
1966 August $675.00

Portrait of gentleman, circa 1760-80
1966 August $100.00

Painting on Velvet, circa 1840
1966 August $275.00

Painting of young gentleman, circa 1780-1800
1966 August $500.00

Still life painting, circa 1840
1966 August $625.00

Engraving, printed and sold by Paul Revere, circa 1770-80
1966 August $390.00

Still life Fruit, circa 1850
1966 August $270.00

Painting of boy, circa 1800-20
1966 October $100.00

Painting of girl, circa 1820-40
1966 October $120.00

Painting of woman, circa 1800
1966 November $75.00

Portrait of boy with toy horse, circa 1800
1967 January $425.00

Pair of ancestral portraits, circa 1820,   1967 January each $210.00

Fully rigged ship painted by Frank Walton,
circa 1820
1967 November $240.00

Painting of gentleman on wood, by Asahel
Powers, Springfield, Vermont, circa 1825
1967 November $325.00

"The Fox Fanciers," Thomas Kelly
1968 January $120.00

Portrait of woman, circa 1830
1967 November $75.00

Trotting cracks on the snow, Currier and Ives
                      1968 January $300.00

A trot for the gate money, Currier and Ives
           1968 January $175.00

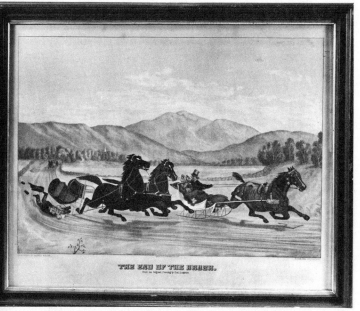

The end of the Brush, Haskell and Allen
           1968 January $250.00

Trotting cracks on the Brighton Road, Haskell and Allen
                      1968 January $170.00

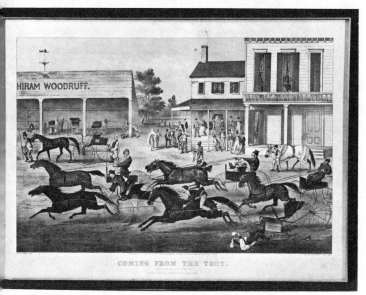

Coming from the Trot, Currier and Ives
     1968 January $220.00

Going to the Trot, Currier and Ives
     1968 January $220.00

A Brush for the Lead by Haskell and Allen
1968 January $250.00

Trotting Cracks on the Road, Currier and Ives

1968 January $220.00

A Stopping Place on the Road, Currier and Ives

1968 January $270.00

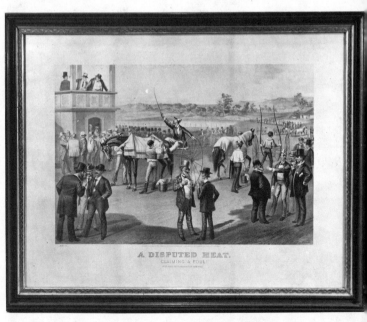

A Disputed Heat, Currier and Ives
1968 January $200.00

Portrait of gentleman, circa 1800
1968 January $525.00

Painting of Clipper Ship in as found condition, Andrew Foster
1968 January $1,150.00

Pair of ancestral portraits on canvas, canvas outlined in gold yellow to simulate frame, circa 1800   1968 January each $1,150.00

Portrait of gentleman with simulated
frame in black and brown paint, circa 1800
1968 January $400.00

Portrait of James Folsom, born July 8, 1737,
circa 1811
a. Inscription on back of portrait
1968 January $500.00

Girl holding pet cat, circa 1820
1968 February $240.00

Oil painting, Village scene, circa 1800
1968 February $130.00

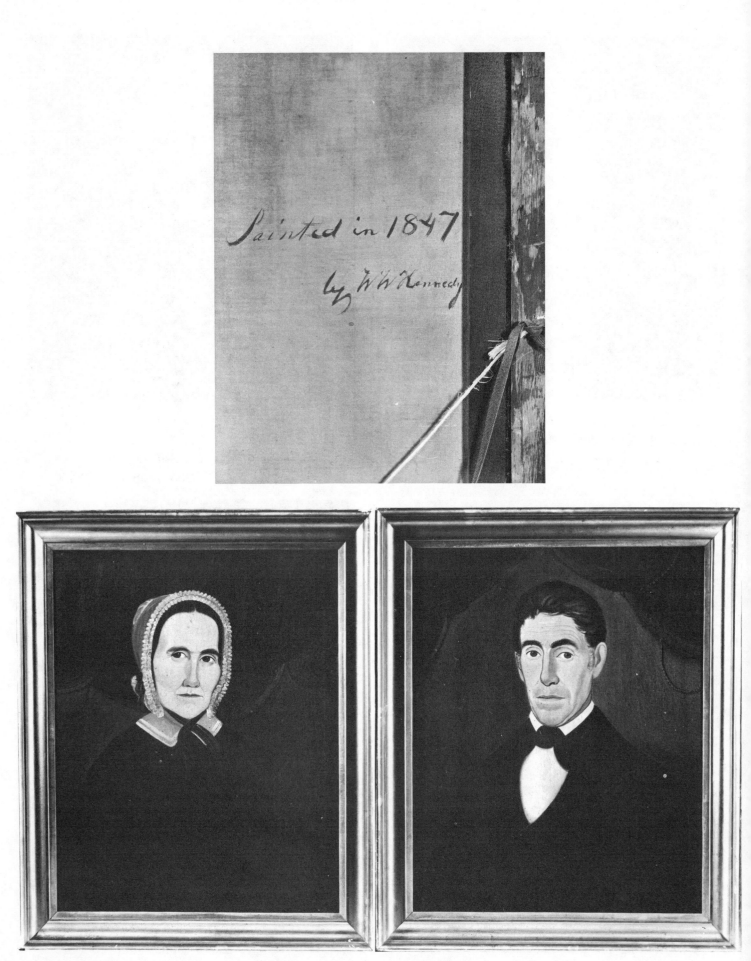

Pair ancestral portraits, painted 1847
1968 February pr. $650.00

Ship painting with American flag, circa 1820,   1968 March $825.00

Painting of sisters, circa 1830-50
1968 February $440.00

Boy with whip, circa 1830
1968 March $325.00

Ancestral portraits, circa 1830-40,   1968 March pr. $620.00

Painting of child with hat, circa 1840
1968 March $410.00

Portrait of woman, circa 1790
1968 April $325.00

Still life cat, mouse and cheese, circa 1860-1875

1968 April $350.00

Portrait of woman holding book, circa 1830
1968 April $360.00

Pair ancestral portraits, circa 1840,   1968 April pr. $360.00

Ancestral portraits, circa 1830, 1968 April pr. $760.00

Clipper ship fully rigged, circa 1830
1968 April $700.00

Pair of oil paintings on wood panels of Dutch landscape, circa 1830-50
1968 May pr. $340.00

Clipper ship painted by Tudgay, circa 1820
1968 May $500.00

Painting of two brothers, circa 1840-50
1968 May $120.00

Painting of a child with fruit in hat, circa 1830

1968 May $225.00

Painting of Ladd Haselton by J. Tolman, circa 1815

1968 July $150.00

Painting of girl, Boston label canvas, circa 1830

1968 July $175.00

Painting on Velvet, circa 1840

1968 July $375.00

Painting of trout, by W. M. Brackett, circa 1864

1968 July $65.00

Painting of gentleman, circa 1830

1968 July $350.00

Painting of Lady, circa 1840-50
1968 August $70.00

Painting of girl with hoop, circa 1800
1968 August $250.00

*Lake "Winnipiseogee", Center Harbor,
New Hampshire, Currier and Ives, circa
1850*
1968 August $200.00

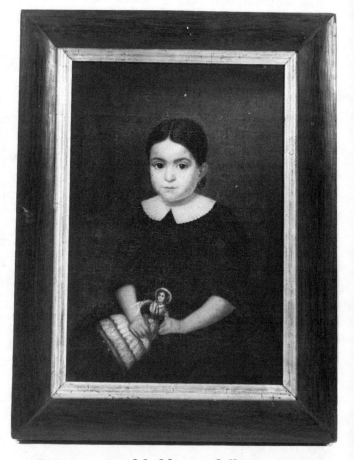

Painting of girl holding a doll, circa 1840
1968 August $330.00

Portrait of girl, circa 1830
    1968 August $110.00

Water color by Clarine P. Gallup of Hart-
land, Vermont, circa 1850-60
    1968 August $55.00

Pair of ancestral portraits, circa 1830,   1968 August each $110.00

Painting of Dutch boy holding a turkey, circa 1760

1968 November $90.00

Painting of young boy, circa 1830

1968 November $45.00

Painting of child and bird, circa 1830

1969 January $500.00

Framed embroidery with Salem, Massachusetts label, circa 1830

1969 February $85.00

Ship Lucilla of Boston, bound for China, circa 1830

1969 February $275.00

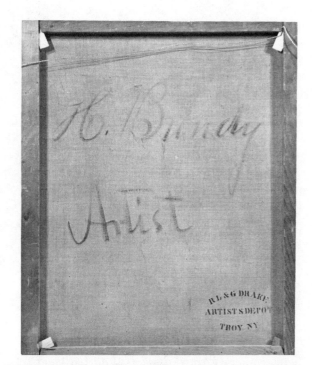

Pair of Paintings by H. Bundy, circa 1847,   1969 January pr. $850.00

Pair of ancestral portraits, circa 1780-1800,   1969 February each $300.00

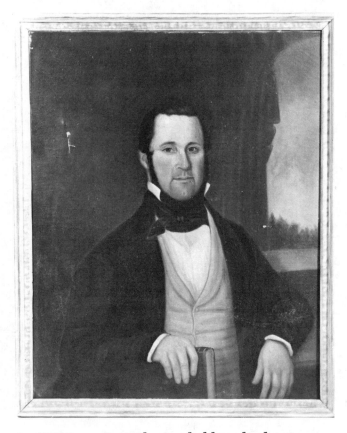

Painting of landscape, circa 1840-50
1969 March $65.00

Painting of gentleman holding book, circa 1830-40

1969 March $290.00

Painting of ship in distress, circa 1850
1969 March $130.00

Painting of Lady, circa 1830
1969 May $225.00

Portrait of young gentleman, requiring cleaning, circa 1830
1969 March $70.00

Clipper ship "Lightning", circa 1860
1969 May $1,900.00

Clipper ship, "Flying Cloud," Currier and Ives, circa 1860

1969 May $1,900.00

*Painting of John Henderson, Esquire, circa
1816*

1969 June $105.00

Portrait of Sally Stedman

1969 September $6,300.00

Painting of a Lady, circa 1820

1969 June $130.00

Portrait of John Quincy Adams Stedman showing back inscription
1969 September $6,300.00

Portrait of Jesse Stedman showing back inscription
1969 September $6,300.00

Portrait of Miss Hannah Stedman showing back inscription

1969 September $775.00

Oriental hanging

1969 October $675.00

Painting of girl holding flower, circa 1830

1969 September $3,900.00

Painting of Ship on wood, circa 1860,   1970 January $500.00

"Bring up the Artillery" by Westey Webber, circa 1870,   1970 January $290.00

Portrait of Gentleman, circa 1840
1970 January $450.00

Portrait of Child with dog, circa 1830
1970 January $240.00

Painting of young lady, circa 1840
1970 January $75.00

English countryside scene, circa 1840
1970 January $150.00

Water color of ship "Monk of Salem", circa 1830-40
1970 January $470.00

Boy grazing his sheep, by Scott Leighton, this artist did Trotting horse paintings from which Currier and Ives copied and printed, circa 1888,   1970 January $425.00

Painting of ship in storm, circa 1840,   1970 January $300.00

Painting of Farmer Plowing, circa 1890,   1970 February $400.00

Prior type painting of gentleman, circa 1830

1970 January $80.00

Painting of Sea Captain holding spy glass, circa 1800-20

1970 January $375.00

Painting of Ship, "City of New York" by Antonio Jacobsen   1970 February $420.00

*Painting of "Ship in Storm" off Thacher
Light, by C. Drew, circa 1800*
                    1970 February $375.00

Painting of child with cat, circa 1830
                    1970 February $275.00

Still life painting, circa 1860
                    1970 February $130.00

Ship painting, circa 1850
                    1970 March $300.00

Painting of girl and rose, circa 1830
                    1970 February $190.00

Painting of young girl, circa 1840
1970 March $165.00

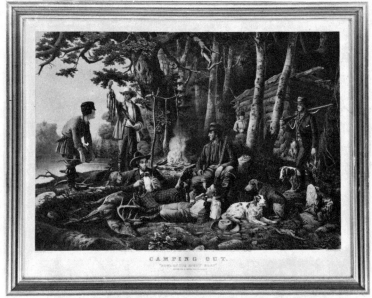

Currier and Ives, "Camping Out," large folio, circa 1860
1970 March $450.00

Portrait of gentleman, Alfred Goodno, Deerfield, Mass., circa 1830
1970 March $650.00

Currier and Ives, "Life in the Woods," large folio, circa 1860
1970 March $425.00

Miscellaneous China, Earthenware, Export, Soft Paste & Collectables

Collection of Luster Pitchers and Bowls
TOP SHELF: *a.* $52.00   *b.* $42.00   *c.* $42.00
SECOND SHELF: *a.* $37.00   *b.* $40.00   *c.* $42.00
THIRD SHELF: *a.* $45.00   *b.* $60.00   *c.* $45.00
BOTTOM SHELF: *a.* $75.00   *b.* $60.00   *c.* $80.00

Pair rose medallion covered vegetable dishes,   1966 March each $90.00

Teakwood curio cabinet
1967 January $375.00

a. Pair of rose medallion urns
1967 January each $185.00

Pair of oriental urns with Fu Dog covers
1966 March each $170.00

Three foot bronze incense burner
1967 January $150.00

Three pieces of blue Fitzhugh　　　　*a.* $375.00　*b.* $ 95.00　*c.* $375.00

Lowestoft bowl, 13" in diameter, circa 1760
1968 March $850.00
a. Interior scene, shows mounted Mandarin warrior

Lowestoft bowl, 12" in diameter, circa 1760
1968 March $850.00

Rose medallion bowl, 20" in diameter, circa
1790-1800
1968 May $450.00

Collection of Mocha:

	BACK ROW			FRONT ROW	
Bowl	$52.50		*Pitcher*		$65.00
Pitcher	$65.00		*Pitcher*		$65.00
Commode pot	$17.50		*Commode pot*		$32.50
Bowl	$40.00		*Pitcher*		$45.00
			Cup		$27.50
			Cup		$45.00

Lowestoft bowl, circa 1780
1968 March $225.00

Lowestoft bowl, circa 1780
1969 March $290.00

Pair of Chinese export covered urns, circa
1780
1969 March pr. $1,040.00

Lowestoft bowl, circa 1780
1969 March $290.00

Pair of Chinese export ginger jars with Mandarin figures, circa 1780
1969 March pr. $600.00

Scrottleware   1969 September
a. Pitcher $420.00 *b. Creamer* $290.00 *c. Bowl* $380.00 *d. Marked Bennington*
Pitcher and Bowl $450.00 e. Tie backs pr. $50.00 f. Pitcher $160.00 g. Sugar
Bowl $180.00

Bennington   1969 September
a. Mug $220.00   *b. Beaker* $35.00   *c. Footed beaker* $150.00   *d. Beaker* $210.00
e. Coffee pot $300.00   *f. Sugar bowl* $150.00   *g. Creamer* $95.00

Bennington items   1969 September
  a. *Coachman bottles*
     1. $270.00   2. $220.00   3. $250.00   4. $280.00
  b. *Book flask* $120.00   c. *Miniature tea pot* $90.00   d. *Toby tobacco jar* $400.00
  e. *Cow creamer* $280.00   f. *Tile* $270.00

Pair venetian wine glasses,   1969 September pr. $18.00
a. Compote $42.00   b. Plates, four $30.00   c. Bone dishes, three $15.00

a. Royal Copenhagen plates,   1969 September each $52.50
b. Royal Copenhagen Forks,   each $ 6.50

a. Parrot $27.00   *b. Three wine decanters* $22.00   *c. Fruit Compote* $45.00
d. Three leaf plates each $20.00   *e. Cauliflower tureen* $15.00

1969 September

Four large pottery crocks 18" - 24" high, $70.00 $50.00 $95.00 $70.00; *circa 1850-70*

Dresden two tier compote
1969 September $120.00

Collection of Steins
$175.00 $30.00 $45.00 $23.00 $110.00   1970 January

TOP SHELF: *Collection of Mocha: a. Pitcher* $55.00   *b. Mug* $40.00   *c. Bowl* $85.00   *d. Pitcher* $140.00   *e. Bowl* $75.00   *f. Mug* $55.00   *g. Pitcher* $170.00

SECOND SHELF: *Collection of Strawberry Soft Paste: circa 1800*

a./g. Pair of plates each $90.00   *b. Plate* $75.00   *c./e. Pair of plates* each $120.00 *d. Tea pot* $275.00   *f. Plate* $80.00

THIRD SHELF: *Collection of Mocha:*

a. Bowl $85.00   *b. Mug* $45.00   *c./j. Strawberry plates* each $100.00   *d. Pepper* $60.00   *e. Mug* $50.00   *f. Cup and saucer* $90.00   *g. Large plate, Whieldon* $100.00   *h. Mug* $35.00   *i. Open salt* $20.00   *k. Mug* $80.00   *l. Bowl* $45.00 *m. Mug* $30.00

Satsuma vase

1970 February $250.00

Collection of Spatterware, circa 1830-40,   1970 February

TOP SHELF: *a. Sugar with cover, blue* $27.50   *b. Mug, house in color* $35.00
c./d. Twelve piece miniature tea set, in green and pink $70.00   *e. Sugar, green and blue* $22.50   *f. Cup and saucer, pink* $25.00

SECOND SHELF: *a. Cup and saucer, fort* $25.00   *b./e. Three piece set, peafowl and green* $210.00   *c. Plate, tulip in green and blue* $50.00   *d. Large cup, peafowl with pink* $65.00   *f. Butter pat, peafowl* $80.00   *g. Cup and saucer, peafowl with blue* $65.00

THIRD SHELF: *a. Four blue plates each* $5.00   *b. Cup, primrose with brown* $25.00
c. Cup, peafowl $18.00   *d. Sugar with lid, pink and blue* $80.00   *e. Cup, rose* $7.50   *f. Cup, schoolhouse* $50.00

BOTTOM SHELF: *a./e. Pair of plates, brown borders and blue cornflower each* $80.00
b. Cup and saucer, blue and pink $80.00   *c. Serving dish, blue border with green and pink sprig* $40.00   *d. Cream pitcher, blue with tulip* $80.00

Collection of Mocha, circa 1820-40,   1970 March

TOP SHELF: *a. Mug* $20.00   *b. Covered cup* $20.00   *c. Mug* $20.00   *d. Cup and Saucer* $17.50   *e. Mug* $10.00   *f. Sugar* $20.00

SECOND SHELF: *a. Covered cup* $80.00   *b. Mug* $100.00   *c. Bowl* $25.00   *d. Mug* $90.00   *e. Footed salt* $27.50

THIRD SHELF: *a. Mug* $90.00   *b. Mug* $45.00   *c. Mug* $40.00   *d. Bowl* $12.50 *e. Small mug* $17.50

BOTTOM SHELF: *a. Bowl* $30.00   *b. Pitcher* $30.00   *c. Pitcher* $75.00   *d. Pitcher* $60.00

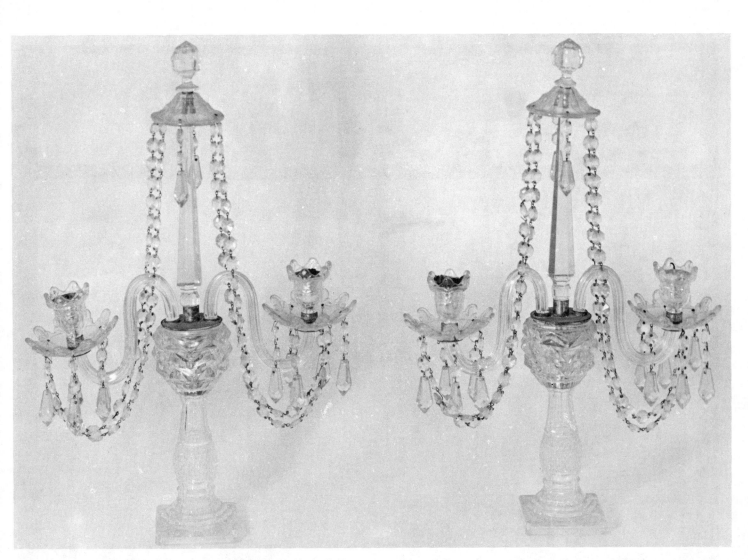

Pair of crystal candelabras, circa 1830,   1964 July, pr. $80.00

a.-c. Pair tall sandwich whale oil lamps with water-fall bases and etched fonts,
  circa 1840,   1964 September, each $100.00
b. Lacy sandwich tray (large), circa 1840,   1964 September $160.00

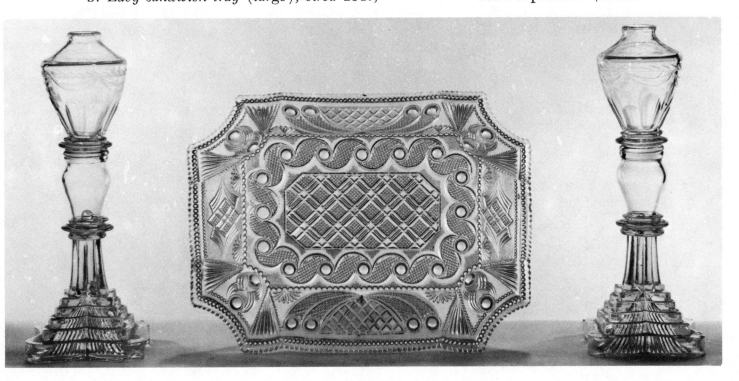

Bottle collection

TOP SHELF: *a.* $20.00   *b.* $22.00   *c.* $15.00   *d.* $30.00   *e.* $35.00

CENTER SHELF: *a.* $45.00   *b.* $40.00   *c.* $22.00   *d.* $35.00   *e.* $30.00   *f.* $20.00

BOTTOM SHELF: *a.* $40.00   *b.* $45.00   *c.* $60.00   *d.* $65.00   *e.* $40.00   *f.* $32.00
g. $30.00,   1968 June

Collection of Amberina:
Small Pitcher $25.00   Vase with applied glass $80.00   Pitcher $130.00   Shade
$25.00   Bottle $60.00   Carafe $50.00   Hat (Not Amberina) $20.00   Fluted Plate
$20.00   Toothpick holder $85.00   Wine $20.00   Folded edge dish or tray $65.00
Stoddard Hat $125.00   Toothpick holder $50.00   Three punch cups, each $60.00
Tall vase $65.00   Vase (Left Front) $25.00   Five punch cups, each $25.00
1968 July

Battersea boxes, enamel on copper, circa 1760-80,　　　　　　　　1964 July

FIRST ROW: $47.50 each

SECOND ROW: ˙ *a.* $47.50　　*b.* $110.00　　*c.* $90.00　　*d.* $47.50　　*e.* $47.50

THIRD ROW: *a.* $47.50　　*b.* $145.00　　*c.* $47.50　　*d.* $47.50　　*e.* $47.50

Group of paper weights. Center illustration shows Millville rose which brought $350.00; others ranged in price from $70.00 to $160.00, circa 1860-80

1964 September

Collection of Miniatures (Note: Eyeglasses show proportion)
Candlesticks pr. $25.00   Piano $27.50   Ship $12.50   Teapot $20.00   Candlesticks pr. $30.00   Seven spoons $20.00   Silver teaset $30.00

1965 August

Foot scraper, circa 1760

1966 July $47.50

Very fine pair dueling pistols with burl
walnut handles, with all accessories
1965 August $430.00

Collection of fire buckets,
a. $40.00   *b.* $37.50   *c.* $85.00   *d.* $37.50   *e.* $130.00

1967 January

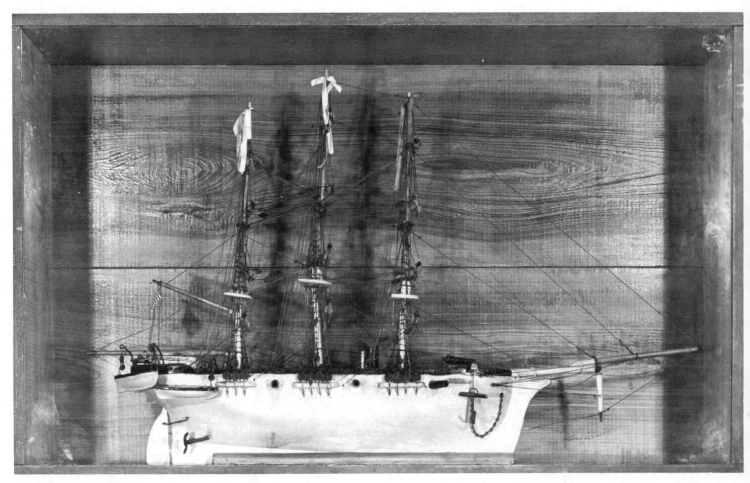

Encased ship model, circa 1830,

1966 November $60.00

Early wire bird cage, circa 1830
1966 August $160.00

Hudson Valley flint lock fowling piece with curly maple stock
1967 January $30.00

Fine pair of encased dueling pistols with powder flask and tools, circa 1800-20

1969 February $375.00

Colt pistol in original box with parts and tools, circa 1810-30

1969 March $630.00

398

Pair decorative columns seven feet high

1969 September pr. $100.00

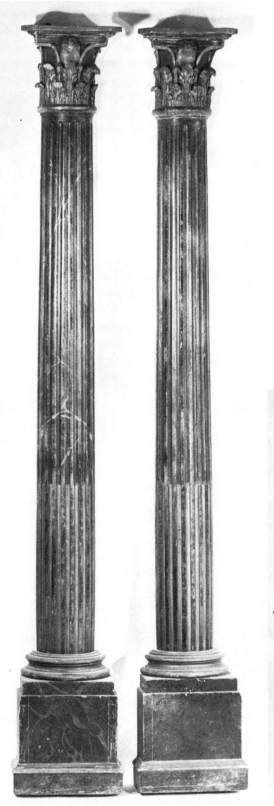

Brass pair scales, circa 1780   1969 September $105.00

a. *Bronze buckets*   1969 September each $20.00
b. *Geese*   1969 September each $42.00

Ship Cronometer, made in New York
1969 September $200.00

Oriental vases,
a. Pair bronze vases pr. $80.00   *b. Cloisonne vase on stand* $170.00   *c. Pair*
bronze vases pr. $45.00

1969 October

a. *Covered Satsuma urns,*   1969 October pr. $620.00
b. *Satsuma figurine,* $380.00
c. *Teakwood stands with marble inserts* $135.00, $160.00, $135.00

Oriental gong on stand
1969 October $175.00

Music box with Marquetry inlay, by
Chevob and Company (Late Baker-Troll
and Company) plays metal disks
1970 February $875.00

Oriental teakwood screen with Canton
China inset 28" high
1969 October $250.00

Collection of fire Americana, circa 1840,   1970 February
a. Hat $25.00   *b. Hat* $25.00   *c. Silver engraved trumpet* $105.00   *d. Hat* $30.00
Insurance Company Marks   *a.* $20.00   *b.* $40.00   *c.* $45.00